Murder, Manners, and Mystery

Murder, Manners, and Mystery

Reflections on Faith in Contemporary Detective Fiction

Peter C. Erb

The John Albert Hall Lectures, 2004

scm press

British Library Cataloguing in Publication data

A catalogue record for this book is available
from the British Library

0 334 04107 4/978 0 334 04107 8

First published in 2007 by SCM Press
9–17 St Alban's Place,
London N1 0NX

www.scm-canterburypress.co.uk

SCM Press is a division of
SCM-Canterbury Press Ltd

Printed and bound in Great Britain by
William Clowes Ltd, Beccles, Suffolk

John Albert Hall

Churchman, chemist, pioneer, soldier, businessman and phil-anthropist, John Albert Hall (1869–1933) emigrated from Britain to Canada in the last decade of the nineteenth century, and made his home in Victoria, British Columbia. He left a legacy to the Diocese of British Columbia to found a lectureship to stimulate harmony between Christian religion and contemporary thought. Colonel Hall's generosity sustained the work of three successive Canon Lecturers: Michael Coleman, Hilary Butler and Thomas Bailey. It also helped found the Greater Victoria Lay School of Theology. Since 1995, it has supported an annual lectureship programme at the University of Victoria's Centre for Studies in Religion and Society.

The Centre for Studies in Religion and Society was established in 1991 to foster the scholarly study of religion in relation to any and all aspects of culture and society, both contemporary and his-torical. Through its publications, fellowships, interdisciplinary research networks and public education programmes, the CSRS provides a rich learning environment for many within the univer-sity and beyond.

John Albert Hall lecturers are outstanding scholars of Christianity who address themselves to the church, the university and the community during a two-week fellowship in Victoria, Canada. Publication of these lectures allows a wider audience to benefit from both the John Albert Hall legacy and the work of the CSRS.

Contents

Acknowledgements

Earlier parts of Chapter 1 were presented as 'Murder, espionage, and other Christian mysteries: contemporary Christian novelists in the secular world', The Revd Howard Bentall Lecture on Education and Theology, for the Chair of Christian Studies at the University of Calgary, Calgary, Alta., 25 January 2000, and 'The Christian novelist in the 1990s', at Trinity Western University, Langley, B.C., 28 January 2000, and of Chapter 3 as 'Two-dimensionality in the work of P. D. James', King's College, Dalhousie University, Halifax, N.S., 29 March 2004. I owe many thanks to my audiences in these settings for additional insights and challenges and am especially grateful for the support of Douglas Shantz, Norman Klassen, Jens Zimmerman, and Paul Friesen, to Louise Gilmour for her close reading of the final draft of the book, and to Barbara Laing, David Sanders, Valerie Bingham, and the staff at SCM-Canterbury Press.

The Hall lectureship offered a unique opportunity to reflect on a number of issues that have engaged me for some time, but little could have prepared either my wife, Betty, or myself for the generous and stimulating hospitality we received in Victoria. The Centre and the Anglican community there are for us inseparable from the graciousness of Conrad Brunk, Director of the Centre, his wife, Chris, the Centre colleagues and associates, Murdith McLean, Leslie Kenny, Moira C. Hill, Michael and Anita Hadley, the 'morning coffee seminar' members, John van Nostrand Wright, now retired Dean of Columbia and Rector of Christ

Acknowledgements

Church (Anglican) Cathedral, and Harold Munn, rector of St John the Divine Anglican Church.

Waterloo, Ontario,
8 September 2005

Abbreviations

BT	P. D. James, *The Black Tower*, 1975
CF	P. D. James, *Cover Her Face*, 1962 (for pagination see *Murder in Triplicate*)
CJ	P. D. James, *A Certain Justice*, 1997
CM	P. D. James, *The Children of Men*, 1992
DD	P. D. James, *Devices and Desires*, 1989
DEW	P. D. James, *Death of an Expert Witness*, 1977
DHO	P. D. James, *Death in Holy Orders*, 2001
DN	Colin Dexter, *Death is Now my Neighbour*, 1996
IB	P. D. James, *Innocent Blood*, 1980
IF	Ian Pears, *An Instance of the Fingerpost*, 1997
MR	P. D. James, *The Murder Room*, 2003
NR	Umberto Eco, *The Name of the Rose*, 1980
OS	P. D. James, *Original Sin*, 1994
RD	Colin Dexter, *The Remorseful Day*, 1999
TD	P. D. James, *A Taste for Death*, 1986
TE	P. D. James, *Time to Be in Earnest: A Fragment of Autobiography*, 1999
UC	P. D. James, *Unnatural Causes*, 1967
UJW	P. D. James, *Unsuitable Job for a Woman*, 1972

Introduction: The Hall problem

The essays that follow are expansions of my John Albert Hall
Lectures, delivered at the Centre for Studies in Religion and
Society at the University of Victoria in the early weeks of October
2004. They arose in an attempt to link the stated intentions of the
Hall lectureship and those of the lectureships' sponsoring bodies,
the Anglican Diocese of British Columbia and the Centre, with a
much less noble purpose: I am an obsessive reader of detective
fiction, and, warned that my professional interest in dead English
cardinals might not have wide appeal, I chose to indulge my
avocation.

John Henry Newman commented somewhere that 'novel reading is an indulgence'. I once understood the adage to mean that
by consuming hundreds of pages of pulp fiction daily one could
be released from years of purgatorial suffering, but even with this
supposed security, I suffered guilt over the unconscionable waste
of time I devoted to reading murder mysteries. Mysteries are
'self-consuming artifacts'[1] – offering yet another means by which
late capitalism hopes to assure itself of its ongoing vitality: the
moment the murder is solved, the book is not only finished, its
calories prove empty, and the hungry reader rushes to purchase
another. That the cost of the volume might have been better
spent otherwise is demonstrated not only in its debased resale
value, but in the speed with which one forgets title, author, and
plot. Too often, within a few weeks, a surfeited reader may
discover that she has previously read her latest purchase, and
Auden's 'guilty vicarage' turns personal.[2] For me one way to

I

overcome the resulting sense of time and fiscal mismanagement was to turn a vice into a virtue and to undertake a study of the murder mystery under the guise of an academic exercise. The Hall lectureship provided the opportunity. My choice of theme required the continuing joy of curling up with even poor books in preparation for the lectures, and, by thus legitimating past vices, may save me some hours in a late-life confessional and a penance I am almost certain I could not bear. In any event, the thought of giving up novel reading for the remainder of my days is unimaginable, and the argument that there will be no fiction in heaven strikes me as inconsistent with the doctrine of the goodness of God.

My task was simplified somewhat in that from the mid-1980s I began to notice a growing use of Christian themes in crime fiction. The phenomenon was not unexpected. G. K. Chesterton, Ronald Knox, Dorothy Sayers, some of Georges Bernanos' and Charles Williams' works, and the 'entertainments' of Graham Greene, among many others had conditioned my eye for it, but I was surprised to find theological topics in popular bestsellers. And yet there they were. Clearly, some of it was a marketing ploy: corrupt Christians, Vatican conspiracies, foreign priests, and unenclosed nuns had assured sales for several centuries[3] and continued in our post-*1984* Orwellian dystopia. Well-worn anti-Catholic rhetoric, often intended more broadly as anti-Christian, regularly served and serves the purpose.[4] Little required change to bring it up to date: supersonic jet travel allowed authors to extend the car-chase, and cyberspace provided a means to broaden an evil enemy's power and, in turn, a hero's intelligence and fortitude. Some of the old characters proved of limited use: the Jesuits, having appropriated liberationist images, no longer proffered the necessary menace to freedom, but Opus Dei numeraries were readily to hand and have been easily conscripted for contemporary needs. At times all that was required for the effect was title alone, announcing a religious theme never taken up in the book itself.[5] And in some cases where traditional cleric mysteries were making a comeback, they appeared to be directed primarily by the editorial adage: 'If short on plot, pop in a caricatured pastor, nun, ex-nun, or woman priest as sleuth.'

Observation is one matter, explanation quite another. It may be that the renewed attraction to anti-Christian themes offers a measure of support for adolescent secular minds seeking warrant for their rejection of parental religious values, or that those same topics provide ongoing masochistic joy for self-styled reformers within particular Christian communities, promulgating programmes that the Church change into something quite unlike itself 'or die'.[6] It may be that committed Christian readers, like myself, gluttonously revel in the assurance of a misdirected hope for beatitude ('Blessed are you when men revile you and persecute you . . .' (Matt. 5.11–12)). It may, of course, also be that there are simpler reasons for the popularity of such works: the delights of self-parody and the joy of predictable retreats from the equally formulaic patterns of modern life.

The increased interest in religious themes that I began to notice in detective fiction from the mid-1980s was not all negative, however, nor was it necessary to reduce all explanations for it to psycho-social ones. A significantly large number of the best books in this genre point in another direction – not to individual or group needs, but to human aspirations. These are by serious novelists: some write from an explicitly Christian position and some from a fully secular one, but all consistently force reflection on the enduring enticement of transcendent presence in some form. The heart appears restless until it rests in something beyond itself, whether it wishes to do so by attacking traditional religious bodies as inimical to a yet more transcendent progressive modernity, or by contending meaningfully with the manifold complexities of modern secular life.

The following essays focus on contemporary writers of detective fiction who take the latter approach. Whether or not they accept a transcendent being or its possibility, all of them struggle in some way with the ongoing fact of transcendental signifiers in human life, that is, with human willing, thinking, and acting beyond itself, and this not necessarily as a need, born from the inability to accept too much reality, but as an element in human thriving. As such their works can be considered 'epics of the modern age', however necessary it is to reduce that genre for contemporary readers.[7] Among the best 'Christian' writers in this respect is the British novelist P. D. James. The biographical details of the life of Phyllis Dorothy James, Baroness of Holland Park, are best presented in her *Time to Be in Earnest: A Fragment of Autobiography* (1999). She was born in Oxford in 1920, moved with her family to Cambridge where she completed her secondary education, and worked briefly in the tax office and at the Festival Theatre. In 1941 she married Ernst Connor Barry White, who served in the medical corps during the Second World War. Following the war she supported her husband (who suffered a severe mental illness until his death in 1964) and their two daughters by work in the National Health Service, with a regional hospital board, and the Institute of Hospital Administration. She was appointed by the Home Office to the criminal department in 1968. In 1960, at forty, she completed her first novel, *Cover Her Face*. The volume appeared in 1962 and was followed by *A Mind to Murder* (1963); *Unnatural Causes* (1967); *Shroud for a Nightingale* (1971); *Unsuitable Job for a Woman* (1972); *The Black Tower* (1975); *Death of an Expert Witness* (1977); *Innocent Blood* (1980); *The Skull Beneath the Skin* (1982); *A Taste for Death* (1986); *Devices and Desires* (1989); *The Children of Men* (1992); *Original Sin* (1994); *A Certain Justice* (1997); *Death in Holy Orders* (2001); *The Murder Room* (2003), and *The Lighthouse* (2005).[8]

I have chosen to centre my reflections on James for a number of reasons, not the least of which is her commitment to Anglicanism, in particular Anglo-Catholicism, the religious tradition of John Albert Hall.[9] My choice of a Christian author is deliberate. Over the past twenty years, the same period during which I have noted an increased interest in religious themes in popular literature, Christianity in Western liberal democracies, including Canada, has faced a marked decline among its regular supporters and a broad indifference to its teaching. What James' novels provide is an environment in which to study this phenomenon directly. Her characters, churchgoers or not, and the situations they are given to struggle in mirror the multiple trajectories resulting from the end of Christendom and the debilitation of Christianity in the Western world, and allow readers to consider more closely the challenges of religious life in an increasingly secularized society. Of the many writers who have taken up this theme, few afford the scope her works do for understanding the place of Christian thought and life in contemporary 'post-Christian' society.[10]

Readers of these essays will note, first, that my discussion is directed to novels and not novelists and, second, that I have not taken up theoretical issues directly. I raise the first issue again in the initial essay, but an introductory comment here is fitting to avoid later confusion. With some frequency members of the lecture audience asked if my reading of the novels was 'really intended' by the author or authors discussed, and my only response then and now is: I don't know. I respect the authors I treat and I suspect that they would agree in large part with my readings, but I am not primarily interested in establishing their intentions. The 'intentional fallacy' debate is now long past.[11] Nor am I here concerned with the broader range of 'postmodern' theoretical issues plaguing literature studies since the 1970s, despite the debt I owe to many questions raised by these. I leave for a later, fuller study the many complex matters raised by those early considerations on literature and religion by T. S. Eliot, Alan Tate (with his compatriots) among others, the limited 'Religion and Literature' or 'Religion and the Arts' interests of the 1960s and 1970s, and the more recent 'theological' approaches, sometimes continuing the thematic studies of the 'Religion and Literature' approach, but more often in search of exploring the literary imagination, literary works, and aesthetic matters generally as avenues for understanding the theological enterprise as a whole: its constructive and instructive roles, often considered in Christian circles in light of the Incarnation, and often blurring the lines between the development of a 'Christian

literary theory' or 'Christian poetics' and 'theological aesthetics'.[12] Throughout the reflections which follow I approach a
literary construct in the same way as I approached marshland as
a child – to puddle in it, to be surprised by toads and turtles and
black snakes, to compare it to other like places and the neigh-
bouring farmland, and now and then to trace one of its many
rivulet sources, never supposing that I could eventually explain
its origins, all its modes of being, or this marsh's particular place
in the intentions of its divine creator. Whether one should treat
'fiction' as 'fact' in this way may be questionable, although it is
always well to remember that both words are formed from the
Latin root *facere* ('to make') and that, as John Buchan once put it
'in these days . . . the wildest fictions are so much less improbable
than the facts'.[13] I do not hold a Romantic view of the novel as a
creation; I approach it as an artefact, the work of an artisan, a
self-existent product, a manufactured mimetic pattern of reality,
deserving respect in and for itself and not for the actual or supposed insights of its maker. The serious novelist is neither a
propagandist nor a clever advertiser; the good novel must speak
beyond its maker's prejudice and its consumer's escapist
pleasures, whether the latter be plebeian comforts or passing
academic theories. A fine corner cupboard by a serious cabinet-
maker serves to highlight many collections, not merely those
envisioned by the cabinet-maker. Respect for the novel, and the
novelist, is manifested first in offering full *attention to*, that is,
waiting on the words of the text (as Simone Weil suggests[14]),
allowing it to speak for itself in its world and the world to which
it alludes, and reflecting on its manifest reality in the same way
as one reflects on human and natural reality generally, rather
than forcing from it the necessary answers from preconceived
questions. The one who waits on a text does not so much bring
questions to it, but discovers oneself pondering questions arising
from it analogically.

A number of such questions are considered in the first chapter.
What is mystery? If mystery fiction offers the reader nothing
beyond the solution of a crime, doesn't it prove itself ephemeral

and self-destructive? Can a writer of detective fiction, then, ever be considered a serious novelist? James proves this is possible; she is the 'serious author' she has consistently expressed the wish to be.[15] Written for a multi-faceted, secular, popular audience and set in a Christian context, her work directs readers to expand the common definition of mystery and to interpret her and other authors' books accordingly. What makes her especially interesting for my argument is that her work marks the mid-1980s shift I have noted and that, in doing so, it offers striking parallels to the work of her contemporary, but expressly non-Christian, writers. The turn is marked in her 1986 *A Taste for Death* and continues in her *Devices and Desires* (1989), both of which when contrasted with Colin Dexter's *Death is Now my Neighbour* (1996) offer a useful introduction to this wider understanding of 'mystery' and to the principles of reading a literary text concerned with religious and theological topics.

James also provides an avenue to explain the popularity of detective fiction at large. Is it simply an opiate for increasingly insecure middle-class minds, struggling to be assured of a permanent moral order? Or does it speak of something at the root of human life? What lies at the origin of the human species? Such questions of crime and faith, of human limitation and fall, are as old as the Genesis telling of Cain and Abel and are revisited in James' *Original Sin* (1994) and Umberto Eco's *The Name of the Rose* (1980) in the second chapter.

The third chapter focuses on the problem of justice. Who is the murderer? This is the chief question in all detective novels: the murder is secondary; the novel's narrative depends on the murderer's elusion of justice, on the killer's ability to replace a crime with a convincingly constructed illusion of innocence, and to escape punishment by means of good manners. The successful criminal must be a consummate artist. But is all art, then, like that of the murderer, based on a lie? Is every work of art an idol, a graven image, shaped to replace a final truth? And are manners simply self-justifying communal forms of self-righteousness, unwilling to forfeit private charity for public justice? The problem, already evident in the Exodus cases of Bezalel and Oholiab, the workmen of the sanctuary, is explicated in P. D. James, *A Certain Justice* (1997) and Ian Pears, *An Instance of the Fingerpost* (1997).

But how is the punishment to fit the crime? Standing as it does in the future, can justice be anything other than retribution, death without hope? What satisfaction can be made for the loss of a human life? A loss is known only when it is known, acknowledged, remembered, and if the one who caused the loss is to be redeemed, that person's memory must be redeemed. How can a murderer ever fully remember killing as a loss? How can a murderer fully confess a crime and experience thanksgiving in final release from the consequences? These are the questions of the final chapter. For the ancients such quandaries were linked with the virtue of piety, first explored by Sophocles in his *Oedipus the Tyrant*, a tale of murder that Freud might not have so badly misconstrued, had he considered Dante's reformulation of murder and mystery in the *Paradiso*. In our own changed circumstances these challenges are intensified, joined as they are to our sense of having lost our common past and our growing recognition that even the memory of the past's death is fading. Whether or to what extent such a death may be interpreted in analogy with homicide is in part the mystery in P. D. James' *Death in Holy Orders* (2001), a work that bears comparison in this respect with, among others, Colin Dexter's *The Remorseful Day* (1999).

There is a further reason for having chosen James and the other authors noted above. Her work provides a useful context in which to treat the announced purpose of the Hall lectureship, namely, 'to stimulate harmony between the Christian religion and contemporary thought'. That directive, shaped by a nineteenth-century mentality, fittingly described the differing apologetic programmes of all parties in the Anglican community in Hall's day. The Low Church, Evangelicals, and the more conservative wing of the Tractarian movement (the Oxford Movement or

'Puseyites') supposed that critical scholarship could prove the Bible and traditional world-views correct against all challengers. Many Broad Church and Liberal Christians sometimes simplistically held that harmonization was best implemented by the appropriation of contemporary thought, and the new turn of Liberal Catholicism within the Anglican High Church announced in its 1889 manifesto, *Lux Mundi*, its 'attempt to put the Catholic faith into its right relation to modern intellectual and moral problems, . . . [to] look afresh at what the Christian faith really means, . . . conscious also that if the true meaning of faith is to be made sufficiently conspicuous it needs disencumbering, reinterpreting, explaining'.[16]

Whichever of these interpretations of the Hall directive one might take, difficult enough as they were to puzzle out in their own time, they prove doubly problematic in the noughts of this third millennium, in which we are faced not only with an earlier generation's questions and concerns, but must face at the same time the radical disjunctures between their world and ours. Where James' work proves especially useful is the way in which it portrays the peculiarities of our own time in which a culture increasingly cut off from its roots must nevertheless attempt to draw life through that source.[17]

A British emigrant to Canada, John Albert Hall was born in 1869 and died in 1933. In his lifetime, despite the Victorian crisis of faith and the challenges of the new sciences, there remained for him the possibility that Christianity could be interpreted harmoniously in its then contemporary setting. In wide regions of the country no distinction was made between the Christian religion, broadly interpreted, and the mores and thought of political society as a whole, allowing persons like Hall and many other Christians, whether Anglican or not, to hold 'the great doctrine [of Hooker] that the state is a person, having a conscience, cognizant of matter of religion, and bound by all constitutional and natural means to advance it'.[18] It was the continuation of the Constantinian model of Christendom. In 1878, for example, when Hall was still a boy and before he arrived in

Canada, the Court of the Queen's Bench in Ontario ruled that the town of Napanee could refuse to provide public facilities for lectures on free-thought, since if they allowed disbelief to be promulgated from a podium in that hall, they would be permitting 'their property to be used for what the law holds to be an illegal purpose'.[19] Nor did the notion that Christianity was central to civilization pass in Hall's life. In the decade of his death, the Prime Minister of Canada, William Lyon Mackenzie King, could still insist that the country's participation in war was part of a defence of 'Christian' civilization.

Such conclusions are no longer possible. In Hall's day Christendom was rapidly approaching an end. He and his associates may be excused for not recognizing its demise and the problems and dangers it raised since the change had come slowly.[20] Already in the sixteenth century, the situation was changing, not only with respect to the relationship between the religious and the secular realms but in other and perhaps more significant ways. Monied economies, the rise of the nation state, the loss of tenure, the advent of mobility, the replacement of traditional rights with legal writs, the exchange of a solid earthly sphere at the centre of the universe for a human eye-ball at the small end of a telescope ever-widening its margins into new geographies and fields of knowledge, the reduction of final cause to pragmatic values, and the turn of the inductive sciences to judging truth on the basis of material and effective causes alone – all these radically restructured secular attentions while the realm of religious life and thought itself was undergoing more serious changes. The primacy of the contemplative life collapsed before that of action: Luther focused the divine vocation within ordinary life and Loyola recommended retreats from the world so as to return to work with a renewed clarity for worldly operations. Earlier versions of love turned downward as well. Where once Dante had travelled out of hell and through purgatory, drawn and formed by beatific love (his Beatrice), Petrarch in the next generation looked only to the stars for distant guidance as he roamed the mazes and the vast fields of memory of this world. Where earlier the divinity of love attracted and recapitulated itself, in the generation following, it served merely as a sign for possible direction. And by the seventeenth century the modern individuated and interior self announced its own bold purposes, setting itself aside from nature as it did so. Thus, Juliet's cry from the balcony gives voice to a modern anthropocentric realm against its cosmocentric and theocentric predecessors: 'Oh, swear not by the moon, th' inconstant moon. . . . / Do not swear at all;/ Or, if thou wilt, *swear by thy gracious self,*/ which is the god of my idolatry,/ And I'll believe it.'[21]

Christians in Hall's day differed from ourselves in another way. Initially the difference does not appear so great. They too had to consider widespread indifference to and the explicit rejection of Christian teaching by their contemporaries.[22] What Hall and his co-believers sometimes failed to understand was that the arguments that self-declared opponents of Christianity promulgated were not always aimed directly at Christian principles. What they often argued against, for example, was not the Christian Trinity, but the newly constructed, unified, and increasingly male-gendered god of Deism. The Deist position is dependent on rational proofs for God's existence, a permanent and universal moral law, and the certainty of an afterlife in which final justice will be meted out. To deny or disprove the existence of God is not necessarily to attack Christianity. The earliest Christians were designated atheists by the Romans and there is an early tradition in Christianity which insists that God is in some way beyond existence. Moreover, the Christian doctrine of forgiveness is effectively anti-moral in the Enlightenment and post-Enlightenment sense (forgiving one's enemy is no way to ensure a just order), and Christianity has never really been very clear on what happens after death – even its Lord responded to a bereaved sister with a paradox: 'though he were dead, yet shall he live' (John 11.25). As a result, in their struggle to offer rational proofs for the existence of God, traditional Judaeo-Christian morality, or the afterlife, Christians of Hall's day harmonized not their own, but a rationalized natural theology with their contemporary culture, the end for which Lord Gifford intended his Scottish 'religious studies' lectureship to serve.[23] The harmonization of Christian and contemporary thought in this setting was and remains a debilitation of orthodox Christianity.

By the close of the First World War Hall may have recognized this in indistinct outline as a flight from authority – wrongly confused with a flight from God[24] – and thus he and his contemporaries began to characterize it as 'secularization' and secured themselves with the hope that however one defined the term, the secular transition was explainable. If it marked the increasing rise of secular political authority over religious spheres, the former, they argued, could be separated from the latter without any detriment; the new turn could be understood as an interference although not necessarily a rejection of the religious orientation in individuals or in the public at large. If it defined a decreasing engagement of the public with church institutions, the pattern could be reversed with some energy. If secularization described the growing presence of some new philosophy, calling all in doubt, including faith itself, one might trust faith to hold firm.[25] All was not lost: there was after all evidence that the religious orientation remained in many forms – as the distant memory of a former age, a comfortable habit, a civil structure even in republics that repudiated any established church, and as inherent in human thriving itself – in the search for a universal answer and for world-wide political unity, manifest, for example, in the wide attention given to and antagonism raised against any image of the unity of humankind, such as a pope or, in a much narrower context, political leaders. Even as privatized, the argument went, perhaps fading religious interests could be revitalized. Apologetics remained a possibility and, in changed circumstances, a requirement as never before.

At the close of the Second World War, however, a new phenomenon was upon Christianity. Since 1945 it has grown ever more difficult to speak of harmonizing 'the Christian religion and contemporary thought'. With Auschwitz and Nagasaki[26] the relationship between Christianity and secular culture changed and nineteenth-century concerns such as that of the death of God, although often cited, proved passé. The fact of these two enemy and supposedly defeated 'cities of man' was not that God was dead, but that he was silent, the problem of his silence proving particularly disturbing within Christian communities. Apologetics, once a defensive tool, now stumbled at its centre. The Christian God is known primarily by his Word, proclaimed by the Church in the preached word and celebrated sacrament, in Scripture and tradition. For Christians, God's Word and the tradition and institution through which it is spoken are co-extensive. By 1945 the churches and their heritage lay as artefacts of a now silent, increasingly meaningless, past. The words remained; the Word itself was silent. What are Christians to do in the face of the unanswered prayers of God's chosen people, the Jews, and of their own petitions as God's Gentile step-children, suffering in the concentration camps of the Second World War and thereafter? At Auschwitz no traditional explanation sufficed. And at Nagasaki, at the centre of the explosion where all particles including sound spread out from the centre, there was absolute silence.[27]

Earlier generations were required to face an announced 'death of God', but there remained enough vitality in the body of Christendom to avoid the implications of such rhetoric. The post-1945 world faced the death of his Word and could do so no longer. The challenge was not that there was no God; the existence of God was left as an open question. The problem was that the Word, if heard at all, appeared distant and unconcerned. The secular no longer stood outside the Christian setting; it had entered it. Thus, in P. D. James' *The Children of Men*, a midwife calls for some evidence concerning God: 'That God exists?' she is asked. 'No.' she replies: 'That he cares' (CM 186).[28] If God is dead, the whole matter of divinity, transcendence, and religious-what-have-you can be ignored by those who wish to be free of it. But so demonic was the fact of Auschwitz and Nagasaki that transcendence could no longer be denied; evil stood incarnated and the realm from which it ascended to enter the flesh was determined as unknowable. Atheism gave way to a-theism – the denial of a God to the decision to live without God, and secularization to *laïcisme*. In this new setting the problem is not so much that church attendance is dwindling or that ecclesiastical matters have increasingly come under secular rule; the problem is that for believers and non-believers alike, 'spirituality' may be righteously asserted, but religious belief is consistently called to doubt, the trappings of the clerical institution and its tradition silenced while at the same time necessarily affirmed for *laicité*'s and secularity's self-definition. To be lay or anti-clerical requires a clerical base against which to contend, to be secular, a religious opposition.

Modes of escape are possible. Non-believers can reify the experience of the silence of God as a brave new religionless world into which we are called and interpret the traces of the past as pointers to desiccated structures of earlier witchery, either transformable or dead. As dead, they are paradoxically considered the innocuous impractical artefacts of a bygone age, permissible for private nostalgic indulgence, but not allowed to public view lest, like infectious vapours of a decomposing corpse, they endanger the common good. Following the traditional patterns of Christian sectarians, secularists can insist that they have separated themselves from the old decadence and have established a renovated, pure, rational 'church'.[29] Secular free-thought is merely old schism writ large, its own brand of fideistic rationalism firmly developed over against what it characterizes as a deluded, conservative or outdated, heretical opponent, and 'righteousness' becomes the common claim and 'reform' the mutual hope of both.

The experience of God's silence changes all such hopes and casts apologetics into a new framework. What it forces on modernity is a recognition that although Christendom may have died politically in almost every modern Western nation, it continues culturally. The silence of God is not to be equated with his absence by either Christians or their cultured despisers; if God were truly dead, one could not speak of or rage against his silence – there would be no silent one to designate. In the modern West, even anti-Christian rhetoric is forced to build its new edifices with or within the collapsed remnants of cathedrals. God is remembered in the remains of the Christian day, sometimes clearly enunciated in acts and institutions, sometimes barely recalled, always present in words, but silent to the times. The purpose of his body, the Church, remains evident in the post-*1984* world, defended by some and rejected by others; its meaning, however, increasingly cannot be grasped.[30]

A passage in James' *A Taste for Death* sums up the matter. The plot of the novel centres on two corpses, that of a tramp and that of a Baronet and Minister of the Crown, Paul Berowne, who prior to the novel's opening has undergone an undisclosed religious experience and begins to make changes in his life that, in turn, precipitate his death. '*What* happened to Berowne in that church?' is the primary question – a 'what' uniting sudden death and the in-breaking of the divine.

> 'Do you believe that something really did happen to Berowne in that vestry?'
>
> 'It must have, mustn't it? A man doesn't chuck his job and change the direction of his whole life for nothing.'
>
> 'But was it real? . . . Was he deluded, drunk, drugged? Or did he really have, well, some kind of supernatural experience, I suppose?'

There is possibility for an answer in the seeker's supposition, but the word of God, the voice of the body of Christ remains silent. For Christians, 'practising member[s] of the good old C[hurch] of E[ngland]', supernatural experiences are 'unlikely', and when asked if they believe in 'God, the Church, religion', cannot give a direct answer, but would have their children christened in any event. 'Why?' one character is asked, and replies: 'My family have been christened for four hundred years – longer, I suppose. Yours too, I imagine. It doesn't seem to have done us any harm. I don't see why I should be the first to break the habit, not without some positive feelings against it which I don't happen to have' (TD 288–9).

It is in this that the spiritual crisis of our time finds expression as a malaise[31] for both Christians and non-Christians. The religious voice continues to speak, but its Word is silent. In Auschwitz and Nagasaki God was silent, but people did *pray*. The devout *called out*, although they were not answered. And religious voices *continue* in our time – including the voices of those who reject any possibility of religious reality (even the 'beyond' of life 'beyond good and evil'), beseeching pessimistically into an unmediated future, their desires for ecological balance or social justice ever outdistancing them.[32] Like Cordelia Gray, James' first formulation of a female detective, such individuals are 'incurably agnostic, but prone to unpredictable relapses into faith'.[33] Condemned to struggle within the confines of a religious voice, at the least of a transcendent hope, they often attempt to avoid the malaise by reversion to a more primitive religion, that of fate. Fatalism is a temptation for the religious as well as the a-religious. In the face of natural disaster, sudden illness, and accidental death, there remains for it only the ironic comment 'That's life', when what is meant, and denied in the very words, is 'That's death'. Before a premeditated murder human limitations and its fallenness cannot be so simply sidestepped. In a premeditated murder free rational human agency proves itself aboriginally sinful and confronts all human hope not only with the close of life itself, but also with the mystery of its own self-deceptive ends and thereby with the religious question in naked form, a form in which the aggressive cynical resignation asserting blunt realities as 'so be it' can be understood only as wisdom's personal *fiat*, 'Let it be.'

But for this exploration we must turn to the essays themselves.

I

Reading mystery:
In the end is the beginning

'[I]n order to make a rather mysterious story as clear as possible,' G. K. Chesterton once wrote, 'it is better to begin at the beginning.'[34] Few readers of detective fiction will disagree: to rush to the last page of a murder mystery destroys the intent of the tale and any joy one might have in it. Crime fiction,[35] in particular, depends on plot, and to leap to the end without struggling through the puzzles in the narrative is like swallowing an apple whole and then hoping to comment on its taste. Every reader knows the delight of engagement with novel pace and style, fictional characters and their development, the expected and unexpected turns in form and formula, and that moment of regret when one realizes that the last page will soon be turned and the joy of this reading ended – that with its final words, the novel dies.

But what of the 'end' of reading? For devoted readers who have grown to love a book, its end is its death. And yet, for devoted readers, the death of novel is always followed by something more than lament. They know that at the close, there is a purpose; in the end, one might say, that is in the death, there is an 'end', a reason for being. Serious novels only offer us full insight when they are concluded; as they end, the reader begins. Almost all of us understand this when we close a novel or watch the final scene of a good film. As we do so, we experience a pause, a brief moment in which we recognize that we now 'know' something we did not know earlier. At the close of the reading there is an instance of wonderment, in which we take, or desire to take, the briefest silence to ponder what we have learned and have not yet assimilated. 'If I read the novel again,' I think to myself, 'perhaps I will grasp this elusive "something",' and on rereading – *Middlemarch* for example – I am driven once again by a new Antigone on the final page back to the Theresa on the first and revisit again 'the number who lived faithfully a hidden life, and rest in unvisited tombs.'

If the heroine of George Eliot's *Middlemarch*, Dorothea, can repeatedly function for readers according to the etymology of her name as 'a gift of God', why should there be any fewer bestowals of grace in serious murder mysteries, and might not the openings for the reader provided at the end of a detective novel serve as a reasonable way of distinguishing good works from bad ones? Only as new life arises from the dust and ashes of death does the old life and its death have meaning. Take, for example, the last page of P. D. James' *Original Sin*. The murderer is dead. Fleeing his pursuers, or, perhaps better, pursuing his own death, he has fled into the marshes. Help has arrived too late by helicopter, and there is little left to be done by either the fictional characters or the reader, except to tidy up and return to the real world. We are left to ponder the situation of two junior detectives, Kate Miskin, and her colleague, Daniel Aaron.

> He [Daniel] stood with Kate at his side until the three figures had joined the pilot and entered the helicopter. The machine roared into life and the great blades slowly revolved, spun into a haze, became invisible. The helicopter lifted and lurched into the sky. Etienne and Estelle were on the edge of the field looking up at it. He thought bitterly: they look like sightseers. It's a wonder they're not waving goodbye.

The three figures, including the senior detective, Adam Dalgliesh, only hint at a trinity in this mechanized ascension, before which stand a few sightseers, not knowing whether to wave goodbye or not, uncertain of the future since no secular ministering angels assure them of a return.

> He said to Kate: 'There's something I've left in the house.'
> The front door stood open.

The stone has been rolled away. There remain only the hints of the guards placed before an earlier tomb. The flames of hell into which that first-century figure descended, 'smeared with blood', offer as well memories of Plato's cave.

> She came with him through the hall and into the study, walking behind him so that he shouldn't feel like a prisoner under escort. The light had been turned off in the room but the flames of the fire threw dancing gules over the walls and ceilings and stained the polished surface of the table with a ruddy glow, as if it had been smeared with blood.

The evidence of what once was remains:

> The photograph was still there. He was for a moment surprised that Dalgliesh hadn't taken it. But then he remembered. It didn't matter. There would be no trial now, no exhibits, no need to produce it as evidence in court. It wasn't needed any more. It was of no importance.

The evidence is of no importance. This is not a world in which absences are recognized and faith required as a result. The modern world is a world of facts, of knowledge, of certitude based on sensual data, rationalized as necessary and when unnecessary, dispensable. It is a world turned upside-down in which ascension images move backwards in time from the end to the beginning – to an open tomb, a body, the blood of the crucifixion, and finally to a lost and hopeless Eden. Daniel 'left [the photograph] on the table and, turning to join Kate, walked with her in silence to the car' (OS 426). As the scene was described and the tragedy more fully explicated by an earlier writer:

The World was all before them, where to choose
Thir place of rest, and Providence thir guide:
They hand in hand with wand'ring steps and slow,
Through Eden took thir solitary way.

(John Milton, *Paradise Lost*, 12:646–9)

We are here at the end, at the final words of the work, and we are now ready to begin to unravel the mystery. A death, the death of Eden, has occurred, and readers are left to choose, with their progenitors, that final mystery: 'Thir place of rest'.

There is no harm done, then, by beginning with the close of P. D. James' *Original Sin*. She, with detective writers before and after her, expect us to begin there. Every murder mystery begins with a death and this one does so as well, although the death marked by the last page of *Original Sin*, like the primal sin of Genesis, marks the reader's own demise: the novel is over, reading is at an end, what is one to do next? Without a death, there is no mystery; in detective fiction, as in life, we begin at the end, with murder, and work back from there. The mystery depends on it. 'In my end is my beginning,' Mary Queen of Scots put it[36] – truth is found not in success, but in the mystery of failure. At the close of *Original Sin* the reader certainly fails. There will be some who cannot hear the allusions to Christian myth and for whom this mystery will be set aside in favour of another fictional diversion. Among these there will be some, so accustomed to the silence of God, that any echo of a divine voice is offensive. Secular literalists, they will defend their state by refusing to 'read anything into a good story'. But there are others, religious and non-religious, non-Christians and Christians alike, who recognize that the inevitability of death and the continual evidence of human willingness to kill opens them, like James' chief inspector, Adam Dalgliesh, to silent wonderment or, in traditional Christian language, prayer.

We know of two places where Dalgliesh prays. Once was in his struggle to discover the murderer whom he has designated 'Cain' in *Death in Holy Orders,* and his experience forces him to think back. The only other time

> he remembered having prayed with passion and with the belief that his prayer was valid had been when his wife was dying and it had not been heard – or, if heard, had not been answered. He thought about death, its finality, its inevitability. Was part of the attraction of his job the illusion it gave that death was a mystery that could be solved, and with the solution all the unruly passions of life, all doubts and all fears could be folded away like a garment[?] (DHO 178–9)

The problem is that the doubts and fears cannot be 'folded away'. The hoped-for end to the mystery of life, Dalgliesh discovers, is not simply solved, and the end he is seeking, strangely enough, he knows only because of a previously heard psalm, pointing back to the beginnings of the universe itself: 'And thou, Lord, in the beginning has laid the foundation of the earth; and the heavens are the works of thine hands: they shall perish, but thou remainest; and they shall wax old as doth a garment; and as a vesture shalt thou fold them up, and they shall be changed; but thou are the same and thy years shall not fail' (Ps. 102.25–7 (Authorised Version); DHO 179).

Dalgliesh, like his juniors Kate and Daniel and an increasing majority of our contemporaries, is not religious in the traditional sense, but, like them, he represents the best in human openness to the mystery of life. Dwelling in the era designated by his initials (AD, *Anno Domini,* 'the year of the Lord'), he remembers, to a greater or lesser degree, a religious language that formed him in part and once formed his forebears more fully. His investigations are thus always compromised: he cannot probe the mystery of life and its end in any straightforward manner. His search is hampered by past prejudices that remain as reminiscences for him and for his colleagues as lingering, forgotten directives, removed from their original contexts, silent, and no longer meaningful. Like the search for the murderer, that for life itself and its meaning is constrained to turn to the past, to undertake an act of retrieval[37] if it is to make any sense of its endeavour.

Reading Christian and contemporary mystery

Dalgliesh's religious difficulty echoes his vocational obligations. In the latter he is called to investigate the voices surrounding him, releasing himself from their intended narratives so as to establish a narrative consistent with the facts. His arrival at the truth cannot be managed without attention to the information told him and yet he must recognize that that information is flawed and at times deceptively offered. The religious words of his past come to him in the same way and are likewise attended to, so as to find meaning amidst the shortcomings and limitations of life, and above all in the loss of life. The difficulty in both the case of the detective and that of the religious seeker is not to lose hope. Four decades ago the Canadian philosopher George Grant took up the problem, concluding his *Lament for a Nation: The Defeat of Canadian Nationalism* with a transference of religious principles to political tradition and then back again to religious tradition. Grant warned his readers against self-pity in the light of the loss of the good, counselling courage for the many 'who have had to live when their only political allegiance was irretrievably lost', and pointing to a 'far nobler' loss than that of a political tradition, one calling for a virtue beyond courage:

> Beyond courage, it is also possible to live in the ancient faith, which asserted that changes in the world, even if they be recognized more as a loss than a gain, take place within an eternal order that is not affected by their taking place. Whatever the difficulty of philosophy, the religious man has been told that process is not all. '*Tendebantque manus ripae ulterioris amore.*'[38]

The Virgilian close to this passage sums up the activities of three differing persons bound together in our argument: there is the detective seeking to unravel the mystery of a specific death, and by analogy, the contemporary religious person attending to the mystery of life as a whole and the reader/critic unravelling the meaning of a text – all, by analogy, 'holding their arms out-stretched in love toward the further shore' (*Aeneid*, Book VI). All are faced with silence and seek meaningful voices within it: the detective cannot hear the victim's voice, silenced by the explanations of the living; the religious person, in a parallel way, must ponder the remnants of a silenced Word, crucified, dead, and buried; and the reader/critic struggles to uncover meaning in silent black spots on a white page. The former two are distinguished from the latter, however, in that they remain open to the silence. As readers we tend not to, believing that just as the author knows from the beginning who the murderer is, so she intends her readers to discover any wider meanings she has structured into her story – her feminism, anti-feminism or post-feminism;[39] her moral perspective, her Christian faith.

We may begin to unravel the problem by considering first the last point raised: the perspective of a Christian writer. Unfortunately, the practice of applying the adjective 'Christian' to the noun 'writer' is a highly contended one in our times, not the least by 'Christian writers' themselves.[40] James once commented on the issue as follows:

> *Are you a Christian?*
> A very bad one
> *A Christian writer?*
> No. To say that I am a Christian writer suggests that I write to propagate the faith or to explain my own spiritual life. I don't. I write detective stories and I write them as well as I can. I love the form, I love the structure, and within that I hope I say something true about human beings, about life. Inevitably my own view of life which is fundamentally religious tends to come through. And it's true that in all the books there is a religious element; for me that's a very important part of life, so that it would be very odd to leave it out. But I never think,

'Look, you're a Christian, you need to make more Christians or better Christians.' That's not the kind of writer I am.

I do the best I can to write well, and in a sense that is Christian. I feel that the gift I have is God-given and nothing for me to be proud of. Also, I have been given the energy to pursue it and given much good fortune. That brings with it obligations and one obligation is to write and one obligation is to write as well as I can.[41]

Her response here is interesting. Many authors (some holding Christian views, some priding themselves as 'lapsed') when faced with the same question endeavour to distinguish their status as Christians from their work as writers, sometimes one suspects out of a need to protect the Romantic view of the artist as the creative genius and often in an attempt to avoid being designated polemicists, proselytizers, propagandists, or the purveyors of dull 'Christian Fiction'. James avoids both dangers. Finding no need to buttress her identity as a 'writer' with synonyms such as secular priest, prophet, 'unacknowledged legislator of the world' (Percy Bysshe Shelley) or 'forger [the pun is possible] of the uncreated conscience of a race' (James Joyce), she can readily recognize her abilities and situation as gifts or divine graces. At the same time her easy acceptance that her religious 'view of life . . . [inevitably] come[s] through' her novels is clearly incarnational and Christian. It cannot be our purpose here to treat in any detail the problem of how an author's 'view of life', religious or not, 'comes through' a work. Suffice it to say at this point that, as a result, a Christian reader/critic cannot be given to reject the search for authorial intention in a literary work (any less than to set aside the search for the historical Jesus); to do so strikes me as ignoring, analogically, the doctrine of the Incarnation and to proffer dangerous possibilities for sacramental and ecclesiological heresies.

But for a Christian reader/critic the author's intention is not the end of meaning for any text, particularly if the work is understood as 'a process more of revelation than creation'.[42] To do so would be to limit the Incarnation in another way by binding the literary work so closely to authorial intention (or a reader's horizon) that the work is reduced to a mere mechanical reproduction of an individual author's psychology or, in parallel critical activities, the image of a culture's social construction. This is not to suggest that the Incarnation occurs solely within 'Christian' boundaries. The point is simply that a 'good' book will speak beyond the author's voice and the explications of an individual reader. No matter how fine the latter, one cannot pretend that there is a parallel between the two, although in some cases there may be. In the present case, for example, I do not suppose that any of the authors treated would necessarily agree with my conclusions regarding the function of their novels as mirrors of contemporary *mores*. The place of the reader/critic is not that of the author, however similar or dissimilar their theological positions or ecclesial communities might be. In this sense the work of the reader, however limited, continues the vocation of the artist, which bears, in Conrad's definition, exact parallels to that of the theologian working within the Christian ecclesial tradition.

. . . The changing wisdom of successive generations discards ideas, questions facts, demolishes theories. But the artist appeals to that part of our being which is not dependent on wisdom: to that in us which is a gift and not an acquisition – and, therefore, more permanently enduring. He speaks to our capacity for delight and wonder, to the sense of mystery surrounding our lives; to our sense of pity, and beauty, and pain; to the latent feeling of fellowship with all creation – and to the subtle but invincible, conviction of solidarity that knits together the loneliness of innumerable hearts: to the solidarity in dreams, in joy, in sorrow, in aspirations, in illusions, in hope, in fear, which binds men to each other, which binds together all humanity – the dead to the living and the living to the unborn.[43]

Conrad's reference to 'mystery' in this passage returns us to our theme. A mystery can be defined in two ways. The first is that common-sense definition of a murder 'mystery', whereby we understand mystery as a puzzle, initially not-understandable, but eventually soluble by rational means, and when so solved, effectively no longer a mystery. But there is another way of understanding the term, that developed in religious traditions, the Christian in particular. In this context the question 'Who done it?' is not the central one.[44] 'Mystery' in the Christian sense, such as the mysteries of the Trinity and the Incarnation, is not something not-understandable, but infinitely understandable. In these mysteries faith is rooted and ever seeks further understanding according to the traditional adage *fides quaerens intellectum*, opening greater possibilities for growth and reflection as the faith-explorer steps forward into the glory and splendour of the mystery in ever increasing awe.

As a result Christian mysteries are never expendable and never concluded. Daily, the ancient liturgies call for a *sursum corda*, a lifting-up of heart in love and praise in the fullness of prayer, begun, as we shall see shortly, when believers are faced by their individual and corporate limitations and are at the same time drawn beyond them.[45] A simple illustration is available in the number 142857. A certain puzzlement arises as one multiplies it by a sequence of numerals and notes its circularity:

$$1 \times 142857 = 142857$$
$$2 \times 142857 = 285714$$
$$3 \times 142857 = 428571$$
$$4 \times 142857 = 571428$$
$$5 \times 142857 = 714285$$
$$6 \times 142857 = 857142$$

Mathematical explanations there are and they fill many pages, but in all they are merely complicated descriptions and do not help us. And our puzzlement increases when we move to multiply the number by the 'magic' number 7:

$7 \times 142857 = 999999$

There are two aspects of our wonderment here. In the first place we recognize our limit; we are faced by our arithmentical finitude. We have memories of nine as a trinity of trinities and of seven as the summation of the divine three and the four of nature (four winds, four seasons, four directions), but we have no explanation for the circulation of the digits or the repetition of the 'magic' nines resulting from the 'magic' multiplier, seven. But there is more to our puzzlement than this; somehow we sense, in our very limitation, the 'more' that 'must' be beyond our limitation – there *must* be an explanation we feel and know as we are drawn out from ourselves into the open mystery. In this sense the mystery is salvific, leading us beyond ourselves, 'saving' us from our individual limitations in our recognition that the number is greater than we are, in our hope that there may be someone outside us who can solve the mystery, and in our desire to know the full mystery of the number, a mystery which we sense is greater than the number itself, since the number lifts us above itself in search of an explanation. A good murder mystery, like other literary works, functions in the same way, leaving the reader at the close to ponder the wider dimensions of the narrative and to live thereafter in the implications of the universal question of 'why' human beings conceive and enact murder, rather than in the localized problem of 'who' committed a particular crime.

It may initially strike one as strange to treat such explicitly theological topics in fiction or in a series of critical essays on fiction, but early Christians would not have found it so. From the first century when the author of Ephesians spoke of 'the mystery hidden for ages in God', they continued to press on 'to *comprehend* with all the saints what is the breadth and length and height and depth, and to *know* the love of Christ which *surpasses knowledge*' (Eph. 3.9, 18–19). Then and thereafter the greatest expositors and defenders of the faith wrote not as modernist Protestants, beginning with the Bible alone 'in its historical context', nor as baroque Catholics, putting off theological debates until all the philosophical questions were answered. In the golden age of Christianity – the brief but sparkling period from the Council of Nicaea in 325 to the Council of Chalcedon in 451, during which all major Christian doctrines and practices developed – the most significant Christian authors were all trained as rhetoricans, specialists in 'the art of persuasion', an art perhaps most closely matched in our time by literary studies. They did not write novels (that genre required another fourteen centuries and the construction of the punctular self within the increasingly anthropocentric biases of early modern Christianity to find its form[46]), but they were fully engaged in literary criticism. Thus, when one turns to Augustine's treatise 'On Christian doctrine', one opens not a dogmatic handbook, but directives on how to read the Bible as a literary work.

Early Christians took it for granted that faith was rooted in mystery and that it was their task and the task of all Christians to lead others into this mystery and to grow in it.[47] Not surprisingly, creedal statements relatively quickly took form as liturgical formulations not doctrinal propositions (*credo* means literally 'I give [Latin: *do*] my heart [Latin: *cor*]' into God the Father . . . into Jesus Christ, his only Son, our Lord, . . . into the Holy Spirit . . .), and the word mystery was speedily transferred to that primal act of prayer, the reading of and meditation upon the Scriptures, the full 'mystical' or 'mysterious' sense of which is not limited to the literal meaning of the text, but is meaningful in so far as, following the directives of the fourfold or allegorical method of interpretation, it leads upward into moral, doctrinal, and eschatological fulfilment.[48] It can result in nothing less if read within the tradition in which it was written and within the writer and the reader dwell.

For earlier Christian writers the distinctive stylistic element of a great work was its *brevitas*, its brevity in the sense of its depth and density: the author of a great work, the Bible above all, so constructed the piece that its meanings could continue to be expanded by later readers according to their own situations and insights into ever-developing truths.[49] Radically condensed, a work of 'brevity' in this sense carries within it an excess of meaning and requires the reader to expand from it – to apply the text beyond itself. It demands expansive reading. Expansive writing, on the other hand, has already completed the task for the reader and leaves her constrained to reduce the text to the outline from which it arose. Such writing turns all its readers back in upon itself; it 'has something to say' and refuses any meaning aside from its own. Expansive writing is literal, uninspiring, and arrogant, finding its own voice and demanding all readers hear it. A significant or serious work of 'brevity' speaks other than itself alone. A grocery list loses all meaning once the requisite items have been purchased, but when words written in another age carry meanings for my situation today, meanings which could not have been known to their writer, we deem them 'inspired'.

All 'brief', inspired, works, however, can be read 'outward', only in so far as the reader has entered or been drawn into their dwelling; one cannot move out, if one is already out. Herein lies the irony of 'brief' writing: one reads it and gains meaning only if one is within it, only if one reads in its tradition, yet one is never limited by that tradition whose scriptures freely unfold increasing numbers of meanings into the future. It is expansive writing that limits and constrains freedom. There was no need to fear the magnificent variety of scriptural truths, inspired, inspiring and ever developing toward the Kingdom of God within the one body of Christ. Thus, Augustine, foreseeing as it were the postmodernist challenge, spoke of the exposition of Scripture in the framework of unbroken charity, commenting: 'Which of us can find out this full meaning, among those so many truths, which the seekers shall everywhere meet withal . . . sometimes understood this way, and sometimes that way.'[50]

Language, then, according to the ancients, does not give us an equivalent of reality either present or historical; it does better than that – it leads us up from reality to a higher reality and at the same time into a deeper reality, to reality's end and to its source. Language in a sense mediates between this world and another. It should thus come as no surprise that the Gospel of John speaks of Jesus as the Word, the perfect 'mediator', or that a Christian commentator should pursue the possibilities inherent in the ancient approach to reading and endeavour to initiate new life by literary means, even such popular means as crime fiction, since for such a reader or writer the whodunit is not a self-consuming artefact – it opens the greater mystery, affording life by fiction.[51] Thus the father and child killer (a theme to which we shall return in the final essay) in James' *Innocent Blood* is described by his wife: 'He liked reading history and biography, never fiction. He lived in his own imagination, not other men's' (IB 77), suggesting that 'salvation' is found in the imagination of others – in coming to grips not with our own thoughts begotten in our pursuit of facts, but in images from others and thus drawing us of ourselves into a reality greater than our own.[52]

The parallel between the detective and the reader/critic is now clarified:[53] both are called to solve the 'mystery', called to read the words as clues pointing beyond themselves symbolically to the full truth.[54] And the work of a detective, like that of a reader is to lag behind, to attend to what precedes:

> If you know what a man's doing, get in front of him; but if you want to guess what he's doing, keep behind him. Stray where he strays; stop when he stops; travel as slowly as he. Then you may see what he saw and may act as he acted.[55]

Chesterton's admonition fits the reader as well as the detective: in both cases it calls for humble waiting and listening to the facts as they lead forward; in both cases one must live in the tradition of the person and world one wishes to understand – incarnation is a necessity, both in a world in which the voice of God speaks and the advent age in which he is silent, in which even the remains of his day call all in doubt.

Reading mystery

Secular and Christian faith in the twenty-first century

A striking and insightful analysis of this struggle with doubt, death, and the traces of past transcendence is Colin Dexter's penultimate Inspector Morse novel, *Death is Now my Neighbour*.[56] The story occurs, for the most part, during Lent, 1996 – the initial murder two days before Ash Wednesday. On Ash Wednesday itself there is a meeting of the Fellows of Lonsdale College against which the plot as a whole develops, but all the characters in the novel appear unaware of this season of penance, and of the death – by error (a vicarious death) we discover – which opens the narrative and the vicarious sacrifice toward which the plot as a whole tends. There are many sacrifices in the narrative, but their offerings bear no resurrection analogies with that of Christ, whose death stands only as an empty signification – the solution comes and the novel ends before Good Friday; there are no allusions to Easter Sunday. A young wife sacrifices her virtue to gain her husband a college headship only to discover that there was no need to do so in any event, and loses not only her husband, but her life. To gain the same end, another wife fails in an initial attempt to silence a blackmailer, murders by mistake her husband's younger lover, and when finally succeeding in collusion with her daughter, finds it all for naught. There are those who suffer for higher causes and with greater nobility. One chapter opens, for example, with the words from Lamentations 1.12, traditionally read within Christianity as Christ's words from the cross as he suffered and died for humanity: 'Is it nothing to you, all ye that pass by? Behold and see if there be any sorrow like unto my sorrow, which is done unto me, wherewith the Lord hath afflicted me on the day of his fierce wrath.' It is indeed nothing. The 'Ecce homo' passage announced, the reader is introduced to Shelly Cornford, suffering the secular crucifixion outside of that of Christ's, waiting late, 'her mind tormented with the terrifying news that her husband had disappeared into the night, never to return'. She hears the key in the door and cries inwardly: 'Come back to me, Dennis!' He has returned, but only

31

to increase her suffering: 'His words before he'd slammed the door had pierced their way into her heart' (DN 253).

An earlier chapter opens with an inscription 'wished to be seen on all churches . . . Important if true', and a passage from the Presbyterian litany: 'Forgive us for loving familiar hymns and religious feeling more than thee, O Lord.' There then follows a depiction of the unbeliever, Morse, who has recently been informed of serious health problems, listening to one of his favourite hymns when his associate, Lewis, enters.

'Sh! My favourite hymn.'
In the silence that followed, the two men sat listening with Morse's bleating, uncertain baritone occasionally accompanying the singing.
'Didn't know you were still interested in that sort of thing,' volunteered Lewis . . .
'I still love the old hymns – the more sentimental the better for my taste. Wonderful words, don't you think?' And softly, but with deep intensity, he recited a few lines . . . (DN 211–12, emphasis mine)

It is all nostalgia. There are religious phrases and allusions throughout the novel, but they are all mere traces of the past glories of a religious tradition and have no meaning beyond the sentimental and the aesthetic. As a final note from Morse to Lewis indicates, there are only two sorts of persons in the world who read them – those with taste and those without it, and neither grasp any transcendent significance: 'For philistines like you, Lewis, as well as for classical scholars like me, this city [Bath] with its baths and temples must rank as one of the finest in Europe. You ought to bring the missus here sometime' (DN 349).

And so life is described: there may be calls to the religious life, but it is a past long passed. One may now lament what once was, may indeed find one's identity in the loss and the memory of that loss. There is nothing more. At the least the centrality of the human rememberer remains, the pride of human endeavour and human potential as a result, and thus the silence is avoided for a time. In spite of all the non-foundationalist chatter the foundation remains, and the radical implications of the silence of God is avoided. 'Death is now my neighbour' – I identify myself by my neighbour, albeit 'death', and 'death' is thus avoided as in Bergman's *Seventh Seal*: Death is a personage whom I can consider as I confront it playing chess.

The texts of P. D. James are quite different. In *Death is Now my Neighbour* shortly after a quotation from 1 Corinthians 13.12 on seeing through a glass darkly, there is a suggestive passage on the religious nature of the quest Morse is undertaking (the solution to the murder and his own mortality) from Housman's *Shropshire Lad*, xxi (DN 235) in whch we have the same approach to death as in Bergman – its aestheticization. Very different is the use James makes of Housman with the key epigram to *A Taste for Death*, acknowledging that while some may aesthetically 'gaze and not be sick', the facts of 'blood and breath' are more problematic: they give a man a taste for death (A. E. Housman, *Additional Poems* (1939), XVI).

This is a call to 'taste' death in all its reality, not to focus on it as an external object so as to avoid direct contact with its reality. The point made in this opening epigram is reiterated on the final page, forcing again a yet greater mystery on the reader. The book opens with the discovery of a horrific murder in a church vestry by Miss Emily Wharton and a young friend; it closes with her return to the scene, finally able to enter the church alone and to recognize both the 'nothingness' of the reality of death in the now empty and silent room, commenting: 'It's just a room, a perfectly ordinary room. There was nothing there, nothing to see.' Having faced the reality of the absence, resulting from death, her gaze is drawn elsewhere, 'to the red glow of the sanctuary lamp, . . . an ordinary lamp . . . fill[ed] with ordinary oil', and from it to the objects whose presence it marks on which she now puzzles: 'the consecrated wafers behind the drawn curtain, what are they?'

For Miss Wharton the wafers too are ordinary '[o]nly thin transparent discs of flour and water which come neatly packed in little boxes, ready for Father Barnes to take them in his hands and say the words over them which will change them into God.' But Father Barnes is silent. He isn't 'any longer in the church'. Like her young friend, and perhaps like God, 'he had gone away', and as a result the wafers 'weren't really changed. God wasn't there in that small recess behind the brass lamp.' In this situation Miss Wharton finds herself, like modern humanity, facing the silence of God. She no longer believes, and, unlike Dalgliesh, silenced but reaching out in prayer at the death of his wife and child and at his inability to solve the mystery of Cain's actions in *Death in Holy Orders*, she cannot pray. But like him, she can remember a small admonition far in her past:

> [S]he remembered what Father Collins had once said in a sermon when she first came to St. Matthew's: 'If you find that you no longer believe, act as if you still do. If you feel that you can't pray, go on saying the words.' She knelt down on the hard floor, supporting herself with her hands grasping the iron grille, and said the words with which she always began her private prayers: 'Lord, I am not worthy that thou shouldest come under my roof, but speak but the word and my soul shall be healed.' (TD 459)

With these words, the novel ends, and the mystery continues. Her words are those of the centurion in Matthew 8.8, adapted as the traditional liturgical response of every Catholic Christian before receiving the body and blood of the Lord.[57] As such, in spite of the awful silence around her, they indicate Miss Wharton's willingness to 'taste' the real presence of the death of the murdered men and of the silent crucified one in whom she hopes for healing. In this Eucharistic openness, for Miss Wharton and for all those in an age without God, there is thanksgiving. Like Mary, she stands in silence, able to identify only with the silence by her own unworthiness and the words of acceptance: 'Let it be.' Like the owl of Minerva that prefigured her wisdom in an earlier age, she can take her flight only in the darkness of a spiritual Good Friday.

Martyrs and murderers: death and the Christian past

The Eucharistic allusions at the close of *A Taste for Death* bind together the two aspects of mystery we have been considering. With a murder, even so idyllic a society as that of the English country house can never return to its earlier quiet peace. The murderer can be found, justice can be executed, but the age of innocence is lost forever, and fictional characters and readers alike are faced at the end of the narrative with a renewed and broader task of detection. The detective, Dalgliesh, is called upon to interpret a sequence of events that have resulted in death. It is his task at the end of the narrative to call together everyone in the community, to take them back to the beginning, and to explain to them what initiated the story they have been required to live. For a detective the specific task, to discover the murderer, requires a fuller account of the circumstances regarding the murder, including the relationships within the community in which it occurred, and of human nature generally. The search for the killer, accordingly, includes a search into the deeper mysteries of life as a whole, and some formation, as a result, of an explanatory worldview for all those caught up in the events. Not surprisingly, such individuals (including Emily Wharton and a myriad of readers, whether committed Christians or those suffering a loss of faith) find themselves piecing their lives together with remembered fragments of the Christian myth. Just as the detective must reconstruct the past, tracing what has occurred through the memories of the community in which it occurred to make a judgement, so the Christian daily confronts the death of Christ at the Eucharist in an *anamnesis*, 'a perpetual *memory* of that his precious death, until his coming again' (*Book of Common Prayer*).

The Eucharistic allusions at the close of *A Taste for Death* likewise direct the reader in his or her search for a solution of this greater mystery. The detective's search for truth is not only carried out in time and memory, but in community. Dalgliesh must search the past but he is not a simple historian, supposedly standing back from the fray, analysing the data objectively, and concluding 'how things actually happened'. From the moment he enters a case, he is enmeshed in a tradition. He must work out the problem in the middle of things, in a story delivered and received according to the interpretations and misdirections of all members of the community, including the victim and the murderer, and the community's ideals of justice, bequeathed from the past and directed to its future perfecting. Peace and quiet does not return to the community once the crime that destroyed it is solved. With murder, a community is irreparably changed. The 'establishment' of justice is something far greater than the re-establishment of a former world. When justice is done, the horizon of the community changes with the truth revealed and justice 'for all' is established with and within the tradition.

In this respect Dalgliesh's search for truth is an analogy for that of Christian faith seeking understanding. In *Devices and Desires* James creates a particularly interesting case for investigating the parallels between these two. The title of the novel, taken from the general confession in the *Book of Common Prayer*, announces the central theme: 'We have followed too much the devices and desires of our own hearts.'[58] Following the devices and desire of one's own heart is especially problematic when seeking understanding within the Christian tradition. In reviewing any past tradition, we are faced with a twisted version of the truth, confused views of justice and many self-justifications that need to be sorted out in the context of the ecumenical order. Herein lies the problem: In a full community there will be different tellings of the tradition, and some so sincerely told that the tellers are willing to die for the truth of their statements. But what if the martyr is mistaken? What if the truth told is a falsehood, the devices and desires of one's own heart that continues on through a community and its tradition, misinforming it as to its ideal formation? The problem is suggested early in James' novel. Adam Dalgliesh is on holiday in Norfolk where he has come to attend as well to the estate of his aunt. He is now alone; she was his last surviving relative. Nor is his isolation solely loss of family. He is a poet, and after four years of silence, he has published a volume, the title of which points into the unknown to a further silence: *A Case to Answer* . . . , not one offering an answer. On his way to his deceased aunt's home he undertakes an errand for an associate and stops to deliver page proofs to an Alice Mair at Martyr's Cottage. James describes his approach carefully:

> No one appeared as he drew up and, before lifting his hand to the bell, he paused to read the words of a stone plaque embedded in the flints to the right of the door.
>
> *In a cottage on this site lived Agnes Poley, Protestant martyr, burned at Ipswich, 15th August 1557, aged 32 years.*
> *Ecclesiastes chapter 3, verse 15.*
>
> The plaque was unadorned. . . . One of the advantages of a religious education is the ability to identify at least the better-known texts of scripture and this was one which it needed no effort of memory to recall. . . . The words . . . had remained with him. It was, he thought, an interesting choice of text.
>
> *That which hath been is now; and that which is to be hath already been; and God requireth that which is past.*
>
> He rang and there was only a short delay before Alice Mair opened the door. (DD 18–19)

The passage raises a number of questions, the answers to which provide clues to the eventual solution of the crime, but also to the larger mystery of the novel with which we are here concerned. Time stands still between the moment Dalgliesh lifts his hand to the bell and the moment he presses it. There is no delay between the two, suggesting that there is no delay between the past and the present, a point that will be made again and again in the novel. Agnes Poley the martyr, the one burned in 1557 at an age close to the age at which Christ was crucified, is present throughout the novel, at times sensed as a lingering ghost, at times not so known, but always present and pointing to the death of the twentieth-century resident in her home.[59] The martyr, it turns out, begets the murderer. *'That which hath been is now; and that which is to be hath already been. . . .'* There is only a short delay between the ringing of the bell and Alice Mair opening the door and casting light on all that is to come.

The place of a destructive past, active in the present, however, is here probed more deeply. James' Dalgliesh has a fuller religious education than Dexter's Morse. Dalgliesh's father was, after all, a clergyman. Even Morse would have recalled the early section of Ecclesiastes 3.3, 4: *'. . . a time to kill and a time to heal . . . a time to weep and a time to laugh'*. But Dalgliesh, unlike modern readers here reminded of their loss of tradition, remembers more; forced as he was, we are told, to copy it out many times, he can quote the 15th verse: *'That which hath been is now; and that which is to be hath already been; and God requireth that which is past.'* Perhaps Dalgliesh recalls the verse because of the final co-ordinate clause. As an officer of the law, he knows that *'God requireth that which is past'* of the detective so that he can discover the murderer, and of the reader so as to open understanding. Perhaps as a clergyman's son, Dalgliesh might also know the confusions passed on in the text by tradition: the Douai/Rheims version of the text promising *'God restoreth that which is past'* – with its implication that justice will be meted out.

But there is a simpler exegesis of the verse for Dalgliesh, one that fits even better with his profession and the knowledge that he has come to in it that criminality appears to be constant in human life – that original sin is inherent in the human condition. The misdirections of the past continue to be passed on to the past's own destruction. As Dalgliesh arrives at Martyr's Cottage he catches sight of an overgrown Victorian rectory and concrete defences from the Second World War, 'seemingly indestructible' like the theology of the rectory, one can suppose, but now 'half-submerged'. And further on 'the broken arches and stumps of the ruined Benedictine abbey gleamed golden in the afternoon sun against the crinkled blue of the sea'. God is here silent, like the Victorian rectory and the Benedictine abbey, in whose ruins a final clue to the murder will be unheard. Overpowering all, silencing all, stands Larsoken Nuclear Power Station. After that, all is emptiness: '[A] few straggling trees, distorted by the wind, struggled to keep their precarious hold in the uncompromising soil,' the result, it appears, of the atomic cathedral itself, 'a grandiose modern monument to the unknown dead' (DD 17–18).[60]

And then, almost suddenly, the reader stands with Dalgliesh before Agnes Poley's Cottage, the home of a martyr over four hundred years dead and yet alive to all about her. The door of the cottage often stands open (DD 119), and Meg Denison, a minor character with major importance, who often visits there, recognizes Agnes Poley's abiding presence in the place where she once lived. 'She is here. Something of her remains,' she admits to her friend Alice Mair, the present occupant. But Alice senses nothing of the past, although she understands the implications of its presence full well and will live to know it directly. To Meg she responds: 'I suppose it depends on your understanding of time. . . . [I]t can go backwards, then perhaps she is still here, still alive, burning in an everlasting bonfire. But I'm never aware of her' (DD 124).

Tragically, Alice will come to believe, the flames of the past will prove everlasting, and Alice Mair dies as a new martyr for scientific method. The difficulty is that, as in the past, so in the present, the victim is the murderer. The past and present coalesce. The abused abuses. The martyr gains posthumous fame and rightly so since she is the martyr of modernity, of the silent, literal, one-dimensional, disenchanted world.

> She went to the stake, apparently, for an obstinate adherence to her own uncompromising view of the universe. She couldn't accept that Christ's body could be present in the sacrament and at the same time physically in heaven at God's right hand. (DD 88)

Agnes Poly is the martyr for science, for clarity of interpretation. She is a heretic in that she reifies language; she kills the word by limiting it. She reads novels one might say by ever attempting to control the meaning, to reduce it by her 'choice' (we do well in this instance to recall the etymology of the word 'heresy' from the Greek word *haeresis* for 'choice') to what she deems the author's intention. She is not open to love the direction of the word, its openness, but rather wishes to control it and the future it could speak into.

Meg Denison understands her. Meg lost her position as a teacher because she refused to switch the letters in 'black', drop one and add another, and refer to a 'blackboard' as a 'chalk-board'. She thus regularly offers 'a small act of homage' to Agnes. '[T]o die horribly for your own common-sense view of the universe is rather splendid' (DD 88), Meg reflects. '[I]f there are ghosts at Martyr's Cottage, they will be friendly spirits' (DD 408) for people like her and yet she must admit that Agnes may have been wrong with respect to 'her earthbound view of the sacra-ment' (DD 88). Meg acknowledges the contradictions in her reactions to Agnes; they make it difficult for her to plant her ideas. She has the same problem gardening. As Dalgliesh pointed out: 'It's a stony soil in which to put down roots.' 'Perhaps that's the kind of soil my roots need,' she responds, acknowledging her humble openness to the difficulties surrounding her. When she comes to say 'her last goodbye' to Dalgliesh, it is an hour later and one of silence. No words between the two are reported. There is truth, but it lies 'between' persons. It is not the posses-sion of either and its power is that 'unspoken', it is one with love, a love 'as devoid of pain as . . . of hope', and a love that allows one who with the enigmatic 'smile of happy surprise' (the smile of the Blessed Virgin on Holy Saturday indicating her assured hope of the resurrection and so delicately transferred by Leonardo to his Giaconda) realizes its reality to face any future evil without fear, to live fully incarnated in the present formed of the past and to continue carrying out those simple acts of silent love and service.

[S]he turned and looked north at the power station, the gener-ator and symbol of the potent and mysterious power which she could never separate from the . . . mushroom cloud, symbol too of the intellectual and spiritual arrogance which had led Alice to murder . . . . And evil didn't end with the death of one evildoer. . . . But that was in the unforeseeable future and the fear had no reality. Reality was here in a single moment of sunlit time, in . . . the broken arches of the abbey . . . . Here the past and the present fused and her own life, with its trivial devices and desires, seemed only an insignificant moment. . . . And then she smiled at these portentous imaginings and . . . strode out resolutely for home. The Copleys would be waiting for their afternoon tea. (DD 408)

2

Why murder?
Rewriting original sin

Why murder? The difficulty with this question is that it includes
a number of questions: What might have led a specific individual
to murder in a particular case? How are we to explain so universal a human phenomenon? For our present purposes there is a
more immediate question: Why is there a literary form centred on
murder? How are we to account for the rise of detective fiction in
the past century and its ongoing popularity in our own? Perhaps
readiest to hand is the 'bourgeois' explanation. According to this
theory the reading public can be divided into two groups, those
attracted to the espionage thriller and those drawn to the murder
mystery. The first group face reality boldly and without illusions.
They are formed by Cold War insecurities, best represented in
John Le Carré's *Spy Who Came In from the Cold* (1963), and are
willing to live in an ambiguous political and human universe. The
second set of less adventurous individuals, the argument goes,
cannot confront a world without meaning, and read murder
mysteries since they provide a solution to a problem and, by
analogy, offer certitude that there are foundational principles in
life and reason for living. Crime fiction, so considered, is an
opiate for increasingly insecure middle-class minds, struggling to
be assured of a permanent moral order.[61]

P. D. James is sometimes interpreted in this light and she herself often writes in seeming support of such an explanation.

Finally there's the solution of the puzzle and this may be why the detective story is so popular in ages of anxiety. The problems of our time seem beyond human ability to solve, and here in the detective story, at the heart of the novel, you have a puzzle and by the end of the story it is solved, not by good luck, not by supernatural means, but by human intelligence, courage and perseverance. That *may well* be the attraction of these small literary celebrations of order and reason in our increasingly disordered world.[62]

James' 'may well' here indicates that she too has reservations about limiting her work in this way.[63] This defence of the genre as providing bourgeois comfort is, after all, an extension of its definition as 'escape literature', and as such avoids the serious questions it raises in the work of James and those giants of earlier generations, above all Dostoevsky and Bernanos. The 'serious' novel, whatever its intended audience, forces entrance into the greater mystery of its theme, pointing to that primal fact in human experience: namely, that human beings have killed and continue to kill one another. Crime fiction insists that the question 'Why murder?' *must* be asked in every form and above all as 'What does the fact that murder occurs tell us about our nature as humans?'

A bourgeois reader simply avoids the question, preferring a few forgetful hours immersed in a 'good' novel, or to rise from the fantasy in the neo-pelagian assurance that '[t]he problems of our time [*are not*] beyond human ability to solve'. There are more sophisticated critical escapes, as well. The journalist avoids all reference to the broader mystery of murder by ignoring the victim with the conventional questions: How? When? Where? and Why? The first reduces murder to its technique and escapes death's reality by promising to unravel the problem through forensic science. The second escapes by temporalizing the incident, the third by localizing it, and the fourth by individuating and psychologizing, the 'Who?' In this final triumph of the therapeutic, the murderer is explained, excused, and exonerated.

For the journalist a 'good' novel is one which most fully integrates its plot according to the four queries. The aesthetic escape takes a similar direction, 'breeding lilacs out of a dead land', focusing on style rather than plot. The aesthete likewise seeks to avoid the fact of murder and its implications by attending to the novel's form, and avoiding the sting of death under the cover of beauty. It is the first move of a decadent society, whether at the close of the nineteenth or the twentieth century: it reduces the novel by a taste so fined down that nothing remains but closure and death in single self-indulgent sensitivity.

Escaping the end, avoiding the mystery

James' work treats the problem of aestheticized murder with regularity. *The Murder Room* structures it into a museum exhibit and covers it behind masked orgies. *Death in Holy Orders* fixes it alongside a painting of doom, hides it beneath a cassock, introduces its 'reality' with Conrad Acroyd, a journalist who has moved from gossip to 'writing a series of articles on murder as symbol of its age', and counselling the detective, Dalgliesh, away from 'brutal battering[s]'. 'You should read detective fiction, Adam,' he asserts: 'Real-life murder today, apart from being commonplace and – forgive me – a little vulgar, is inhibiting to the imagination' (DHO 6–7). In *Original Sin* the murderer himself is an aesthete, a poet who, inspiration long lost, reads at the burial of a victim a Wilfrid Owen poem that shadows slaughter with allusions to sea-changes that turn dead eyes to pearls and leave others (who cannot interpret the poem as his confession) 'wondering a little at his choice': 'I am the ghost of Shadwell Stair. . . . I am the shadow that walks there' (OS 54).[64]

But whatever form of escape is chosen, all avoid Ackroyd's definition of murder as 'the unique crime' by transferring it and the genre that treats it into a 'symbol' or 'paradigm of its age' (DHO 7) without allowing the question to extend beyond a particular age. All novels, however, even the most expendable murder mysteries, require a response. An escape, in the strict sense, is not a response but an avoidance of such. Indeed, the escapes here outlined are means for avoiding reading itself. Reading is always a moral act, demanding judgement and establishing the basis for co-operative free decisions at the same time. In the response elicited, readers know themselves able to respond. Reading proves us response-able, able to respond and thus responsible moral creatures. To ignore this or to attempt to escape it is, in the case of the murder mystery, the equivalent of quietly burying the body, covering up the murder, and fulfilling the murderer's objective by eliminating all evidence that the victim ever existed. Murders do not attempt to deny victims rights or life, but existence itself. An empty tomb, unlike an unmarked tomb, is no tomb: it does not argue for resurrection; it demonstrates that no life ever was. According to the well-known legal tag: *Habeas corpus.* You must have a body, and therefore the cry of the Magdalene: 'Sir, if you have carried him away, tell me where you have laid him, and I will take him away' (John 20.15).

Whatever form of escape an author or critic might choose, that choice marks the death of the novel being read, by closing its possibilities. If the detective in a crime novel should ignore the death, there would be no possibility of discovery. The same holds true for a reader as detective/critic. Murder necessitates a review of the past and an interpretation of past events. Murder, death itself in effect, makes a past as we seek an explanation for it, and the solution to a murder thus requires a detective with historical skills, who allows the dead to speak while the living restructure their private truths in light of the victim's death. Only by investigating the end, the limit, can one ascertain the truth of the beginning and the meaning of what lies between beginning and end.

In detective fiction the solutions to present crimes are found in their origins. Every murder is 'original' – there is no other like it since we consider every human being unique – and yet murder is a single category, arguing that every murder can be traced to a single origin. The search to solve the unique mystery in any detective narrative is a search at the same time to solve the mystery of the one unique human narrative. For the Western Christian tradition (in which crime fiction, the secular included, is written and read) and in the Christian tradition especially these two are linked as particular and universal. At the beginning and the end of the Christian narrative is a murder – the murder of a particular first-century Jewish preacher, known to his followers as fully man, the summation of humanity, the 'Son of Man'.[65] Christianity is the greatest murder mystery ever told, calling for each of its readers to assess the written and reported evidence, discover the killer, and see justice done.

Trace back the Christian narrative in search of the killer and there at its origin stands Cain, the first son of man (Genesis 4.1). Cain is the first post-Edenic human actor and his first act, the original human act, is to slay his brother. It is not Cain's own act. It has its origin in the actions of his parents who desired to be like gods, to be their own creators, to establish their own beginnings and ends. Cain recognizes that this is impossible. He has parents and cannot be his own creator, but if he cannot create, he can at least be *like* the gods – he can imitate them. *Mimesis* comprises the original temptation, although not first an imitation of another person, but imitation of the gods. *Mimesis*, the imitation of another person is mere copying, a making, a *poesis*, poetry or fiction, and always demonstrates the imitator's limitations, her dependence on originals to imitate and materials to construct. To imitate the gods, however, is to imagine another possibility. To be like the gods is to be equal to them, and if the imitator must implicitly recognize that his constructed fantasy is but fiction, he can at least revel in the pretence of creation, and if, like his supposed divine colleagues, he cannot create life, he can prove his equality with them by taking it. The corporate height of such action is the blasphemous attack on the Resurrection at Nagasaki, three days after the initial full glorification of human power with the dropping of the first atomic bomb on Hiroshima.

The murder of Abel is the fulfilment of original sin since it marks the destruction of what was in the beginning the original human life, namely life in community. Primal human creation, according to the Christian narrative, is social. 'Male *and* female created He them,' the Genesis text reads (1.27), a point empha-sized in the pleonastic retelling of the story in which the Creator, after consistently praising the goodness of the creation, for the first time utters a negation regarding it: 'It is not good that man should be alone' (Genesis 2.18). For the author of Genesis the point bears repeating: 'Male and female he created them; and he blessed them and named them Man when they were created' (Genesis 5.1). Humanity exists as a diverse but unified social creation; the first manifestation of human fallenness is the destruction of that unity.[66]

Cain is a kin-slayer; murder is never simply that of an indi-vidual. It always entails the murder of society itself in that society precedes the person. Consider the etymology of the term 'per-son'. 'Person' comes from the Latin word *persona*, a mask, worn by an actor to indicate his or her character. This is not a mask in the sense of a cover, but a mask as that which defines an indi-vidual's place in society. If I am asked: 'Who are you?' I respond: 'I am a husband, a father, a grandfather, a teacher.' I know who I am in light of my place in a social setting. I am the mask I bear. I am a husband, father, grandfather, teacher. I am who I am because I have a wife, two daughters, a son-in-law, a grand-daughter, students. The community defines me, I am not an iso-lated will contracting with others to make a society; the society precedes me. Without students I am no longer a teacher; without a wife I am not a husband – my daughters, son-in-law, and granddaughter precede my person. I *am*, that is, I have an identi-ty as a father, for example, because I have two daughters. Only an incarnate God can make the temporal claim 'Before Abraham was, I am' (John 8.58), although the Trinity is always personal, known as Begetter and Begotten, Proceeder and Procession.

For our personal being, each of us, then, is dependent on others. Thus in a simple aside, Talley Clutton in *The Murder Room* comments: 'We work together, we see each other frequently, sometimes every day, we talk, we confer, we have a common purpose. And at the heart of each of us is the unknowable self'

(MR 65). Our being is first and foremost social, and therefore a murderer effects death in three ways: the death of the one he kills, the death of the social order in which that other lives ('Murder corrupts,' Dalgliesh comments in *The Murder Room*: 'It's a contaminating crime' (MR 179)), and the death of the killer's own 'self'. Murder is co-extensive with suicide, and with damnation. Depending as we do on others for our identity, if we kill another person, by that act we lose our identity and thereby die, and at the same time are identified by the death of the victim and are thereby dead. Our victim's death is our death.

For Cain the divine warning to his parents is fulfilled: Having eaten of the fruit of the tree of good and evil, he knows death. But his knowledge is more than simply the knowledge of the death of his brother, Abel. So completely does Cain destroy all trace of Abel that even God must ask its location: 'Where is Abel your brother?' (Genesis 4.9).[67] Cain's response is an honest one: 'I do not know.' So deeply has he buried the body and so fully has the earth taken it that every location marks its decease and all ground is cursed for this tiller of the soil. Each time he digs to plant a seed, he re-enacts the burial of his brother and his own identity as a killer and a dead man. The tragedy is that he does not choose to dwell under the mark of mercy and the promise God has given him. The last words the Lord speaks to Cain are promises of protection. The Lord's last actions for him are the protective marking of Cain as God's own. But Cain, marked and thereby offered a renewed possibility of identity – an identity as chosen and marked by God rather than a kin-slayer– 'went away from the presence of the Lord' (Genesis 4.16). He heeds not the voice of the Lord and, in a deliberate attempt to avoid the curse of a fugitive and wandering life, as a person without existence since without any social structures by which to define himself, Cain establishes a city within which he might hope to maintain personal identity. The problem is that the city has no foundation. It is dependent on Cain's own progeny, named after his son, and perpetuated in a genealogy, some of whom raise cattle in imitation of the dead Abel, and the rest of whom commit themselves to the aesthetic life, 'play[ing] the lyre and pipe' (Genesis 4.21), but in their imaginative productions are able only to rephrase catches from the last words uttered to their race by a now silent God, prophesying their city's destruction at their own hands. Once promised divine protection, they must now reform the promise as their own according to their own taste and beauty, seeking justice on their own terms:

> Lamech said to his wives . . .
> '. . . Hearken to what I say:
> I have slain a man for wounding me,
>   A young man for striking me.
> If Cain is avenged seven-fold
>   Truly Lamech seventy-sevenfold.' (Genesis 4.23–4)

It is all in vain. The race of Cain has no future. God appoints for Adam another child, Seth, in place of those who had left the presence of the Lord. 'At that time men began to call upon the name of the Lord' (Genesis 4.26). For Cain and his race, God is dead. His descendants cannot, at least will not, call upon him. In his attempt to be like God, Cain initiates that act characterizing the original sin of humanity that has and will kill God by refusing to respond to his Word and insisting on a residence in ultimate silence. By refusing to respond Cain is enslaved, abusing his ability to respond and thus losing his freedom. His original act will be recapitulated on Calvary's mount, when the nominal darkness, certain of its own established urban security, will have no option but to kill the Word of God, the pure active verb by, through, in, and to which alone all are called to their full identity.

Following openness: *The Name of the Rose*

The now commonplace complaint against catholic Christianity[68] as a closed system, narrowing human potential and limiting 'openness', found theoretical supports even prior to the postmodern revolution of May 1968, in a number of writers, one especially interesting since he continued his argument in detective fiction. In 1962 Umberto Eco, Professor of semiotics at the University of Bologna, published his essay, 'The poetics of the open work', in which he argued for a 'poetic theory or practice of "the work in movement"', recognizing '"openness" as *the* fundamental possibility of the contemporary artist or consumer', establishing 'a different status for the artistic product in contemporary society . . . and pedagogy . . . . [T]he situation of art has now become a situation in the process of development. Far from being fully accounted for and catalogued, . . . it is an "open" situation, *in movement*. A work in progress.'[69]

The implications of Eco's argument for Christian readers of crime fiction were made fully clear in his *The Name of the Rose* (1980; trans. 1983).[70] It is an historical novel, set in the early fourteenth century, featuring a Franciscan sleuth, Friar William, and his Benedictine associate, Adso of Melk. The setting is the break-up of the medieval and the beginning of the modern world. The papacy, that great symbol of catholic spiritual unity, is in Avignon and now a plaything for a particular nationality, the noble ideals of the Franciscans are disputed between two warring factions within the movement, the truths of nature are set over against those of grace, individuals are set to seek their own ways over against communal values. The story itself is located deep in the past. Like the solution to the murder, the truth of the tale must be retrieved by the reader from an English translation of an Italian translation, according to the introductory statement to the book, of notes taken from a lost nineteenth-century edition of an eighteenth-century edition by a French clerical scholar of a fourteenth-century Latin manuscript written by a German. Meaning fades in the layers of interpretation of past texts.

The setting is a monastery at the centre of which is a labyrinthine library – the greatest collection in Christendom. It is filled with secret entrances and exits, known only by the chief librarian, Jorge, who is losing his sight and protecting the last remaining copy of Aristotle's supposedly lost book on comedy. A good conservator and curator he protects the volume with his life and will kill to protect it, but at the same time, as a deeply conservative Christian and offended by the turn to modernity, he fears the book's survival and protects it from all readers. In good medieval style, the central action of the book takes place in seven days, on each of which there is a murder – murders which William attempts to solve by noting their parallels to events in the Book of Revelation. On the night of the seventh day, William confronts Jorge, the librarian murderer, in a secret room in the library. There at last he sees the lost manuscript that Jorge has poisoned so that the person reading it and licking his fingers to separate the pages will be killed. The book kills; the book is poisoned – but William wears gloves.

The mystery is solved, the murderer known, but for William one mystery remains: that of Jorge's motivation. A typically modern man, William seeks finality, not by expanding his vison and exploring the ever-extending ways of God, but by focusing on the psychological underpinnings of the new centre of reality, the individual. Why, of all the books blaspheming the name of God, did Jorge choose this one? For the modern anti- or non-theistic secular mind, the answer is expected: the turn to nature is a turn in the right direction and, having been undertaken, demonstrates the frivolity of any upward gaze toward trans-cendentals. Jorge, a figure of the dying past, must attempt to substantiate a lost cause. As he puts it:

Every book by that man [Aristotle, the Philosopher of nature] has destroyed a part of the learning that Christianity had accu-mulated over the centuries. The fathers had said everything that needed to be known about the power of the Word, but then Boethius had only to gloss the Philosopher and the divine mystery of the Word was transformed into a human parody .... Every word of the Philosopher, by whom now even saints and prophets swear, has overturned the image of the world. *But he had not succeeded in overturning the image of God. If this book were to become . . . [sic] had become an object of interpretation, we would have crossed the last boundary.* (NR 473; emphasis mine)

William cannot understand Jorge's argument. As a traditional Christian Jorge does not deem the power of the Word closed; it remains a power within the tradition of the Fathers. The Philosopher's book on tragedy (the *Poetics*) states the obvious. Interpretations of the work simply lead the interpreters more fully to understand their own fear and pity, and through the grace of the drama, their shortcomings. Catharsis may eradicate fear and pity, but in so doing offers a purer nature by which one may 'seek grace hereafter'. In itself the comic is not dangerous for Jorge. William recognizes this. The in-breaking of laughter is an *in*-breaking, a mark of grace, a joyous opening in which human beings see their shortcomings and their newly offered ability to stand above those limitations in laughter. The problem arises for Jorge when the comic becomes an object in a text interpreting comedy. Objectivized, it now falls under human control and is open to interpretation, and the last boundary is crossed beyond which there are no longer any horizons by which to make judgements on any matters: interpretation with its infinite possibilities, its ultimate openness, its ever deferred meanings, destroys all meanings. This is modernity, and this Jorge wishes to avoid. William may well define Jorge as the Devil in this respect (NR 477), but Jorge, whether or not he understands Francis fully, understands the complexity of the case:

> 'You are worse than the Devil, Minorite,' Jorge said. 'You are a clown, like the saint who gave birth to you all. You are like your Francis who de toto corpore fecerat linguam . . .' (NR 477–8)

For Jorge the tragedy comes when human beings appropriate the laughter-creative functions for themselves, becoming clowns and not the clowns *of God*, and making all of nature (*de toto corpore*) a mere interpretation (*linguam*). The tragedy of the tale, the tragedy of modern life, is not lost to William, however. Jorge remains the Anti-Christ but he recognizes the force of the librarian's argument. As William states the matter:

Jorge feared the second book of Aristotle because it perhaps really did teach how to distort the face of every truth, so that we would not become slaves of our ghosts. Perhaps the mission of those who love mankind is to make people laugh at the truth, to make truth laugh, because the only truth lies in learning to free ourselves from insane passion for the truth. (NR 491)

We are the slaves of our own interpretations and all that is left for us to love is 'mankind', playing the god before it and calling it to laugh finally at its own inability to reach any truth by interpretations. The student, Adso, will not accept so pessimistic a closure to the tale. He insists that William did follow the clues properly and unravel the plot.

'There was no plot,' William said, 'and I discovered it by mistake.'

What of the signs? Adso asks; Surely they were true and pointers to the truth? But any hope that might arise in his question is refuted by the master:

I have never doubted the truth of signs, Adso; they are the only things man has with which to orient himself in the world. What I did not understand was the relation among signs. I arrived at Jorge through an apocalyptic pattern that seemed to underlie all the crimes, and yet it was accidental. . . . I behaved stubbornly, pursuing a semblance of order, when I should have known well that there is no order in the universe. (NR 492)

For William, the Nominalist who holds to the truth of signs but not to realities beyond them, '[t]he order that our mind imagines is . . . like a ladder, built to attain something, but afterward you must throw the ladder away, because you discover that, even if it was useful, it was meaningless. Er muoz gelichesame die leiter abewerfen, sô er an ir ufgestigen.' One must cast aside the ladder at the same time as one rises up upon it. The Eckhartian adage holds and seems to point to an openness before the majesty of God, but William's fideistic protest is the first step toward the modern denial of the divine: 'It's hard to accept the idea that there cannot be an order in the universe because it would offend the free will of God and His omnipotence. So the freedom of God is our condemnation, or at least the condemnation of our pride' (NR 492–3), he says. To this assertion Adso can only conclude that 'affirming God's absolute omnipotence and His absolute freedom with regard to His own choices [is] tantamount to demonstrating that God does not exist'. William's ironic response is the second step, this time toward the modern degradation of the dignity of the human person, confusing Adso even further and allowing him to conclude only that with the death of order, the death of God, and the death of truth, there is no 'possible and communicable learning any more' and, it is suggested, because humankind cannot bear such reality, the depraved will form authoritarian structures in which the learned can 'no longer communicate what [they] know because others [will] not allow [them] to.'

'At that moment,' the reader is told, 'a section of the dormitory roof collapsed with a huge din, blowing a cloud of sparks into the sky' (NR 493). As a grown man, Adso revisited the scene and collected fragments that remained. The collection, he tells us, was 'the result of chance and contain[ed] no message'. Indeed, he does not even know if the text he has compiled for the reader contains a meaning. The gardens of Babylon have passed, the snows of yesteryear are melted and the only assurance of life he has is that '[t]he earth is dancing the dance of Macabré; at times it seems to me that the Danube is crowded with ships loaded with fools going toward a dark place'. His beginning, he tells us, is soon to be before him in his end, and the great mystical openness of the abyss is a closed nothingness: 'Gott is ein lauter Nichts, ihn rührt kein Nun noch Hier' (God is pure nothing; no now nor here stirs him). Nothing can link one word to the next in the absolute silence: 'stat rosa pristina nomine, nomina nuda tenemus' –

The first rose stands in name, we hold but naked names (NR 501–2). The silence of God, of meaning itself, reigns supreme and authoritatively.

Original Sin: Christian closure?

In James' *Original Sin* the reader is introduced to strikingly similar but differently directed themes. The action centres in an institution, a publishing firm, located in 'Innocent House', overlooking the stream of life that passes by behind them and here too the solution to the murders is preserved in archives. The archives point back however to an Edenic location, to an original innocence, and not forward, as in the Eco novel, to an apocalyptic end. Dalgliesh 'reasoned', like Friar William, 'that the motive for this crime lay in the past and that the missing evidence could be evidence in writing' (OS 400), and sent his junior colleague, Daniel Aaron, to ferret it out. He discovers the solution to the murders by playing the historian, searching the archives of the firm.

Throughout the episode, Daniel's activities offer analogies for theological reflection. Discovery is a combination of chance (grace) and hard work (co-operative free will). He undertook the archival investigation partly as 'a self-imposed penance', out of wounded pride over an 'earlier blunder' (OS 397), and he continued it partly because he 'preferred a job to have a defined and tidy ending' (OS 395). By chance he comes upon an old *Book of Common Prayer* and for no particular reason pages through it. By chance an autobiographical fragment from the distant past (September 1850) falls from the book. It is the confession of a murderer, albeit one very long dead. Francis Peverell was so obsessed with building Innocent House that he killed his wife for her money to complete the task and managed a perfect crime. His act was never discovered but on his deathbed he confessed as 'justice to her *memory*' and then set up a *tradition* – each eldest son who inherited the House thereafter is to pass on the secret to the next. The chance discovery, whether relevant or not (and

Daniel thinks it is not – 'But it surely had no relevance to Gerard Etienne's murder' (OS 389)), gives Daniel enough incentive to keep going and by chance again he comes on another bundle. It slips from the shelf and in reassembling the papers his eye falls on the word 'Jew', attracting him because of his religious tradition to read further and solve the murder. The second pack of evidence, a proposal for a book entitled *Original Sin*, begins in 1942 and culminates not in a text but with a photograph. It is all by chance (it is only by chance that the murderer did not destroy the material) and not so: the room is uncomfortable, the task for the most part dull, and yet, albeit not with the best motives, Daniel perseveres, making the best of what chance delivers to him.

Although alone, Daniel works on the past within a tradition, unaware that he is doing so. 'He had no sense that the ghosts of the unquiet dead were the watchers of his solitary, methodical search' (OS 387). He puzzles over the prayer to commemorate the Gunpowder plot, and having parted ways with his own Jewish tradition, he never fully explores the relationship between the two pieces of evidence he had come upon and, not considering the implications of 'original sin', makes a self-destructive decision on the basis of origins that he might otherwise have avoided.

Whether her individual readers will reflect more closely on the two documents and avoid like calamitous decisions, James leaves open. Written in the framework of traditional Christianity *Original Sin* avoids closure, unlike the postmodern *The Name of the Rose*. It is Eco who follows the old-fashioned pattern of saving the solution of the murder to the very end, reducing the parlour gathering of the suspects to whom he can explain the facts for the unwitting reader. Indeed, Eco as the supreme 'open' writer ironically closes further thought for his readers. He explains at the close not only the solution to the murders, but the solution to what I have suggested marks a good novel: for Eco even the mystery of life is 'closed.' All the answers are given in the typical modern 'moral' – the final question is a necessary answer: 'Do you mean,' [Adso] asked, 'that there would be no possible and communicable learning any more if the very criterion of truth were lacking, or do you mean you could no longer communicate what you know because others would not allow you to?' It seems that there are two choices here and thus a further mystery, but there is really only one: communicable learning is no longer possible and humanity will shift to authoritarian structures to avoid the fact. James is very different. The ending of her novel opens as we have seen earlier into deeper mystery, leaving the reader 'open' to grapple with what might initially appear as the Nothingness (*Nichts*) faced by Adso, but promising, as Meister Eckhart proposed, that in that human nothingness there might arise *Etwas*, Something.[71]

Something, according to the Christian tradition, can arise only in silence. 'Unless a corn of wheat fall in the ground and die . . .' (John 12.24). Beside James' Daniel, Eco's Friar William looks like the conservative judgemental Jorge whom he attacks. In her work the Jacob–Esau story is reframed. Daniel is the younger son, always needing to earn parental love, and not having the birthright directly from his parents, he doesn't 'believe in it any more'. The favoured elder brother in a sense doesn't believe it either, but his perspective is different from Daniel's. He remains with the faith: 'There are some beliefs it is worth dying for and that doesn't depend on whether or not they are strictly true.' In Judaism as in Christianity, the words and forms continue. The difficulty for Daniel is that he understands this argument only too well.

The ghosts of the past that oversaw Daniel's work in the archives were those of his own ethnic and religious tradition as well as that of the broader world in which he finds himself – the dead generations who had heard the story of the Innocent House founder's perfidy, the ghost of the tradition of the *Book of Common Prayer*, the Christian past, as well as the 'moving army,' the Jewish 'Church militant' with whom he is bound. His name implies no less: he solves the crime 'alone' and as the full expression of his people, the prophet in exile (Daniel) and priest in the wilderness (Aaron). Phylogeny recapitulates ontogeny in this later age in which God can no longer be heard, but even among the deaf the fragmented signs continue to hold possibility. The knowledge of original sin, whether fully comprehended by Daniel or not, is a knowledge of his origins, admitting that one is a part of the whole:

> Why must I define myself by the wrongs others have done to my race? The guilt was bad enough; do *I have to carry the burden of innocence also*? I'm a Jew, isn't that enough? Do I have to represent to myself and others the evil of mankind? (OS 129; emphasis mine)

For Daniel and Christians at large the answer to these questions is clearly 'Yes.' For Eco's Adso and for William it is 'No.' For the latter two an individual is separable from a socially contracted group, can ascribe the sins of the past and present to others, and thereby, in a reverse of Feuerbach's projection theory of divinity, maintain the delusion of personal virtue against a corrupt mass. Daniel's 'iconoclasm' (as we will see in the following essay) is different: he seeks to define himself knowingly aside from his origins, and in a flight from his past he loses his vocational integrity and the situatedness he thought possible in a secular world.

Like Eco's work, James' too treats the problem of signs: it takes place, not in a monastery (where the rule is supposedly silence), but in a publisher's house (the main purpose of which is to produce words). Original Sin (the concept, not the novel) is a 'book' – it is divided into sections which parallel the murder and the book: there is a 'Foreword to Murder', the 'Death of a Publisher', a 'Work in Progress', and the 'evidence' appears 'in writing', before the last section: 'Final Proof', which readers, Daniel among them, are called to 'proofread'. The final proof is in writing, the text a continuing incarnation, told by James with the deepest respect for her readers and thus offering no explanations, allowing the readers the freedom like Daniel to follow through to discovery in archival collections, preserved in however fragmented a form. Jamesian Christian *écriture*, writing (if one may so play with the once popular adage) supersedes the confident postmodernist *parole*, the speech of William and his associates, preaching, as ironically as they wish, their own certitudes.

In *Original Sin* the solution is in the past – Dalgliesh has thought it would be – whereas in *The Name of the Rose*, the solution is in the future and the future we behold is the death of the author, Adso, who at the close gathers only the traces of memory and fades into a myriad of meanings without exit. His tragedy is that he has collected the past but not grasped the origin, the message of Eden, in and through which, according to the Miltonic phrase, we must make our 'solitary way'.

In James' works there are solutions as text is allowed to be interpreted – the texts open into silence. In Eco there are but traces of silence – openness is considered only in the fabrications of the human voice. Eco charges, prosecutes, and judges. In James murderers confess and in the humility of the confessional (the very opposite of the closure that it seems to imply), speaking into a dark unknown silence, the human voice recognizes in the acknowledgement of its personal and corporate culpability, its ability to respond to the worst and best of what it is and can freely be. In *A Certain Justice*, for example, Janet Carpenter seeks to construct her own justice, after the death of her granddaughter at the hands of the killer who had been freed from a previous charge by a clever lawyer. The murder and its tragic repercussions lead her to formulate and carry out her revenge. Her action begins when her daughter, the last person linked with her in the tragedy, commits suicide and, being 'relieved of the need to try to care and comfort' another, she recognizes that she has lost her faith:

> I don't mean my Christian faith, that High Church Tractarian tradition of sacramental worship in which I had been brought up and in which I had always found a natural home. I no longer believed in God. I wasn't angry with Him, that at

least would have been understandable. . . . I just woke up one morning to the same griefs . . . and knew with certainty that God was dead. (CJ 308–9)

As a result she is aware, not 'of regret, only of an immense solitude and a great loneliness. It felt as if the whole living world had died with God.' Thereafter, carefully and patiently she developed her plan, engaging a criminal to help, discovering that she cannot consult with him in a local church: 'I found, despite my loss of faith, that I had a reluctance to use a sacred building for a purpose I knew in my heart to be evil' (CJ 325). It is a small matter, but one which indicates much about her character and her situation. She has had a faith to lose, and there is no indication in the narrative that she regains it. God remains silent for her. And yet, at the moment in which she sees her enemy destroyed, she concludes falsely that it has been her doing and knew the liberation of revenge, 'letting go of [her] obsession'. At that moment, at the moment that '[w]hat had seemed an act of appalling desecration had become one of liberation', she 'faced the truth. I had conspired with evil to do evil. I who had lost a grandchild by murder had deliberately put another child into a murderer's power.' She had paid a psychopath to corrupt the daughter of a woman she hated, and recognizing 'the enormity of the sin into which [her] obsession had drawn [her]', enacts the ritual in which she had been formed, confesses her nothingness as a sinner, and accepts her responsibility. In that acceptance, not only does she know that she is able to respond, but she plans to complete the ritual act by responding and in doing so, in a final act of love for the one she has harmed, bring about her own death. Had she not died, it was her intention to take a necessary seven days of silence 'to be alone', in a secular retreat of sorts before deciding what to do with the rest of her life (CJ 328–9). Even though she will die, there is a sense that the spiritual Good Friday has passed by and she enters a sort of Marian Holy Saturday, during which, having returned to the religious formulae that shaped her, she has no need to speak or explain and can rest at ease in her knowledge that love might well have salvific ends, even if initiated by false ones.

It is Dalgliesh who, after reading the letter with his colleague, Kate Miskin, remains silent. She is the one to break it. The reason she does, and the further silence she must await, we leave for the moment.

3

Justice and good manners:
When presence is pretence

'Somewhere is better than anywhere.' Flannery O'Connor wrote, 'And traditional manners, however unbalanced, are better than no manners at all.'[72] It may initially seem strange to begin a discussion of justice, the primary motivation of all action in a crime novel, with a comment on manners, but there is much to link the two. There is a long-standing critical approach that interprets the detective novel within the genre of the novel of manners, that is, the depiction of a closed social setting (of manners – often a country-house 'manor', the homophone significant in this case) in which all is balanced and into which the murderer enters, displacing the balance that must then be re-ordered by the solution of the crime, the punishment of the criminal, and the establishment of justice for a return to 'proper' society.[73] Some change does occur, of course. The persons touched by the crime and its solution return to a just and justified society with a matured sensibility. The manor and their manners have the same 'appearance' as before the events, although in the new setting there is a possibility of distinguishing the illusory and the reality.[74] In this context justice is understood in terms of manners, that is, of *mores* (propriety, courtesy, proper behaviour) and this, in turn, of morality. Law, in this setting, is a 'natural' formulation of manners and the directive for a practice of virtue by which the individual adjusts and lives morally in compliance with the social setting. '[C]rime is . . . an individual act, a breaking out of convention.'[75]

Justice and good manners

The English Country House Mystery, so popular from the golden age of detective fiction, began to fade as a structure and all but disappeared by the mid-1980s.[76] This is not to say, however, that the crime novel was no longer classifiable as a novel of manners thereafter. My argument is that by that decade we do not have a rejection of the novel of manners in itself by either James or others, but rather an expansion of it. In its earlier form society was looked at from the outside; it was possible for the author to take the stance of a secular literary anthropologist, to stand back and judge the morality and justice of the older mannered society. What the post-1984 novels indicated was that neither author nor reader can get outside the picture: we are the manners; 'appearance' is all there is. The problem was how to make judgements within it, and the old division, whether true or not, between readers of detective fiction as cowards desiring certitude that the end of life is rational, and espionage readers who recognize that it is not and cannot be, is overcome, the former flowing into the latter. There is a hint of this in James' comment in her *Time to Be in Earnest*:

> The crime novelist . . . needs to deal with the atavistic fear of death, to exorcize the terror of violence and to restore at least fictional peace and tranquillity after the disruptive terror of murder, and to affirm the sanctity of human life and the possibility of justice, even if it is only the fallible justice of men. A distinguished writer of novels of espionage like John le Carré is as much fascinated by *personal treachery and betrayal* as he is by the shoddy international bureaucracy of spying and the dangers and excitement of the chase. Espionage is his internal *as well as his external world*. (TE 137–8; emphasis mine)

Persons in this fiction are, reiterating the argument of the former essay, *personae* or masks. Such plots implicitly oppose modern versions of self-definition that turn from the outer boundaries of the individual inward, that insist that there is a self with distinctive talents within, a freedom straining against social norms to be released, and that the true is the interior, the exterior *persona* a false mask by which the individual projects a self-deluded or deliberately deluding illusory facial image on the world. As novels of manners they recognize that the appearance is the reality.[77] Their characters exist and define themselves within outer boundaries. The difficulty is that many such novels, a number of which we have already considered, also implicitly accept the version of self-definition denied in their narratives, and to overcome the problem shift, in the way in which much of modernity does, to a fatalistic schema – we are the playthings of the gods, the gods of our modern world understood as 'shoddy bureaucracies' and social and genetic determinants, against which humanity is called to battle unreservedly, claiming rights and questioning all proposed responsibilities. Against the inevitable temptation to cynicism and pessimism, the only hope, it appears, lies in coincidence. As an earlier mystery writer once put it:

> In an age swamped by mechanistic physics and mechanistic psychology, the only rock left above the surface is coincidence – beautiful, anarchistic coincidence. In a society that bows down and worships at the altar of statistics, coincidence is the only one remaining manifestation of a higher Providence.

One could expect no better statement from a character who views the place of the publisher's office as not offering 'any strong conviction of reality . . . How could it, living on such an unsolid commodity as words.' The character here is appropriately named, Nigel Strangeways, the sleuth in Nicholas Blake's (pseudonym for C. Day Lewis) *End of Chapter*,[78] a novel from the late 1950s with striking parallels to James' *Original Sin*. Here too the murder takes place in a family publishing firm, the Thames flows by in the cadences of T. S. Eliot, there is a difficult woman writing Romantic novels, there is a play between investigation and book production, and the criminals in both cases, attempting to right past wrongs, die in the attempt to escape. The parallels make the many differences between the two novels more noteworthy, and among these the most significant is their endings in which Strangeways, after a chance miss with death himself, is assured in the final words of the novel 'You're a lucky chap.'[79] Coincidence and luck need no further investigation – one can simply move on to face the next unknown, having solved the most recent one. What James' fiction puts before the reader is the mystery beneath the luck, the fragility and goodness[80] underlying it in all those eternals breaking in upon the person, the other faces that define one and the many inexplicable manifestations forming life itself – 'the extraordinary thing', grace.[81]

As a result James' fiction offers an opportunity to reformulate theologies of justification according to which Christianity from its beginnings understood salvific personal identity. In the six-teenth century Catholics were divided from Protestants, for example, as forensic models of grace replaced medical ones. According to the older, Catholic model, human beings lie in sickness and can be healed only if visited by a physician (the mediator Christ and his Church) who, diagnosing the disease, provides the correct medication and directions for its use. The sick person must then co-operate with the physician, continuing the medical and exercise regimen to grow in health and holiness. In the newer Protestant version human beings are criminals of capital crimes, and coming before a righteous judge, are gracious-ly declared innocent (another has already suffered the penalty for them), free to leave the courtroom, according to Luther's adage, *simul iustus et peccator* ('at the same time justified and a sinner').[82] The difficulty with the division is that the New Testament offers no real way out of the argument, the Greek word for justice and allied words (*dikai-*), being used both in legal (forensic) texts and in those treating medicine and ethics, and pro-viding the religious groups developing from both a rich base for theological insight and growth.

We can begin to approach the works of James on this topic by noting how the two models are linked in the work of the American Catholic author, James Lee Burke.

The opinion of certain people has always been important to me. Most of those people . . . have been nuns, priests, Catholic brothers, and teachers. When I was a child the good ones among them told me, I was all right. . . . As an adult, I still believe that we become the reflection we see in the eyes of others, so its important that someone tell us we're all right. That may seem childish, but only to those who have paid no dues and hence have no question mark about who they are, because their own experience or lack of it has never required them to define themselves.[83]

Luther might have wished for no better description of his theology of human glory in the description here of those who need no justifying voice from beyond them, nor of the theology of the cross in the struggles of those awaiting the redeeming voice, even had he struggled with the ecclesial mediators through whom, Burke indicates, assurance came and the American novelists' conclusion on the need for human action immediately following this reflection: 'I had to go back on the other side of the Divide.'[84] In its secularized Western version, however, Protestant theology rapidly offered necessary props a very different assurance: the rising modern concern with the individual free, willing self, its human rights, justice as established by rationally constructed and interpreted written law, instrumental reason, the new inductive sciences, and definitional truth based on observable evidence. Over against this anthropocentric centre lay material chance and the metaphysical realms of fate. In the novel of manners the traditional Catholic model makes its return, focusing on the nature of the person, human dignity, its obligations, morality,[85] and the justice of a traditionally established social fabric, driven not toward knowledge as power, but the love of wisdom, and offering against chance, choice, response, and response-ability. In this realm 'nothing about murder is private' (MR 329). The decision to take a life cannot be judged in terms of the monetary value of the loss or explained as a psychologically or biologically determined effect. The crisis for justice here is not the actions of the socially maltreated who act out their abuse in public; rather, it is the more frightening demands of the solely self-directed sociopath who rejects all sense of public behaviour and for whom the voice of God is fully silent. 'One of the most interesting problems for the modern writer', James once commented, 'is that there is no longer any accepted philosophical or religious standard against which to judge private morality.'[86] And yet one must work out one's life in public:

> What I was trying to do, of course, was to use the well-known conventions of the detective story in order to write a true novel about the human condition, about men and women, in particular under the appalling search light of a murder investigation. And also, I suppose, something that I feel true about, about humanity and about the conditions in which these people live. In a murder investigation you see all the sorts of carapaces that people build up round themselves to protect themselves. In a sense you can say in presenting ourselves to the world, we all create our character to a certain extent. And then all that is turned around because no privacy is left. It is a terrifying procedure which reveals the truth about them.[87]

The theology of human glory will collapse, denying all possibilities of self-justification and forcing an open review of the emptiness before one. When God no longer speaks, the last horizon fades and with it the lost markers for human identity.

Iconoclasm and justice: the case of Daniel Aaron

This enigmatic aspect of late twentieth-century life as one faces 'the difficulties of compromise and the imperatives of choice'[88] pervades the lives depicted in James' novels.[89] Although much attention has been given to her major characters, her minor ones are in some ways the more interesting. It is in their voices that one often gains the most important insights. Of these the two most striking figures, struggling with the silence of God, are Kate

Miskin and Daniel Aaron, whom we met at the close of *Original Sin*. Daniel, as we have already seen, represents the first generation, forgetful of faith, the 'lapsed', the collapse of the traditional religions from within. Kate is of the next generation, the one orphaned from religious life; so silent are the words and acts that she cannot understand them, much less reject them.

We have already met Daniel Aaron, the exiled prophet and latter-day priest, seeking a centre to live by while struggling with the one he has in part discarded. His tragedy is, as we have seen, that even though he has lost his past, he cannot lose it ('A Jew wasn't even allowed his atheism') and in this confusion of voices, the demands of human solidarity as he perceives them overwhelm his commitment to justice, the principle on which he has endeavoured to create a new life as a police officer. Because he fails to mediate between the two, he loses both, and is replaced in the later novels by Piers Tarrant, a new Peter, the apostolic rock on which new generations of hedonistic but civilized secular successors will be founded, the theologian atheist, who holds a university degree in a subject he chose for its form while deaf to its content.[90]

As we have already seen in *Original Sin* Daniel comes on the solution to the crime in the archives of Innocent House by chance and hard work (salvation by grace and free will). The first confession in the Prayer Book holds the real source for the solution to the novel's mystery, a source left for the reader to reflect on even after the novel ends. The first evidence is an *autobiographical fragment* from far in the past. The second culminates not in a text but with a *photograph*. There are texts associated with the photograph (the last is June 1989), but they merely point to the photograph; the photograph is the final solution, and has a striking effect on the sleuth. As James describes it:

> He put the photograph back in the envelope and the envelope in his pocket. . . . He put out the lights and unlocked and relocked the door. . . . Each action was deliberate, portentous, as if each had a unique value. He took a final look at the great

domed ceiling, plunged the hall into darkness, set the alarms
. . . and left Innocent House, locking the door behind him. He
. . . smiled ironically at the thought that he, resolved on *the
unforgivable perfidy, the great iconoclasm,* could still be
meticulous about the things which didn't matter. (OS 402;
emphasis mine)

The object of Daniel's resolution requires a full explication.
His 'iconoclasm' – this is one of the few places in which James
uses the term – is the destruction of all that makes him an officer
of the law: he has decided to act not as a police investigator but
as a jury and judge and declare the murderer innocent – or at
least to warn him that the evidence has been found. By so doing
Daniel's iconoclastic action is a destruction of the modern liberal
democratic icon of justice, the principle by which he is to live. He
is perfidious in his rejection of the justice system he has been
called to serve. And his action is unforgivable; it is a sin against
the holiest spirit of his and modernity's most recent god. For
Daniel justice is absolute. In this sense he follows the pattern of
Sonia Clements, another character in the novel who, like Daniel,
is self-destructive. As her sister, a nun who must know the ironic
etymology of Sonia's surname, 'mercy', puts it: 'Sonia [once]
replied [to me] that justice had nothing to do with time. We
shouldn't allow ourselves to be dominated by time. If God is
eternal, then His justice is eternal. And so is His injustice.' The
statement was made during a discussion of an article in a
Victorian periodical that told of the suffering of a thirteen-year-
old who, exhausted from overwork, fell into an open fire and
died in agony:

> The story affected my sister powerfully. She said, 'So this is the
> justice of your so-called loving God. This is how he rewards
> the innocent and the good. He wasn't satisfied with killing her.
> She had to die horribly, slowly and in agony.' (OS 275–6)

In Sonia's argument, like Daniel's, justice replaces God as
Sovereign. There can be no wavering regarding its essence for her

or him. It is certain, sure. There are no poorer forms of it, no certain, lesser, or other kinds, dependent on the limitations of the justice system or human creatures as such. It exists out of time; there is no statute of limitations and therefore no mercy. Warning the murderer that evidence has been found or destroying the evidence is not an act of forgiveness, but a decision to justify the act against the express principles of the system and, by making such a 'choice' (again, as in the case of Agnes Poley, note the etymology 'heresy' from the Greek for 'choice'), to reject the system as a whole, to deny its function as an icon and to undertake the role of an iconoclast.

The ironic tragedy for both Daniel and Sonia is that they do not come to recognize that if one rejects the God of one's fathers, if one rejects the primary icon, one is left only with idols, whose presence and their present is pretence – that is, an object pretending to be holy, but in fact mere stone. Daniel bears the name of the one who would not bow down to idols as well as of the one who first created them. Giving up one aspect of his heritage, itself an icon of the one true God, he is driven to perpetuate the sin of Aaron and make justice, a golden calf, to replace it. It is not his Jewishness that marks him as the opposite of Dalgliesh, the cleric's son – his initials, DA, reverting the other's, AD, the one closed on his own truth and the other, however wounded and puzzled, open in 'the year of the Lord'. He is not an iconoclast when he thinks he is. In his decision to act in opposition to the system of justice, he destroyed what was in effect not an icon, but an idol, and by so doing he may yet find redemption in a return to his Jewish heritage, the icon he had once broken. It need not be a matter of belief, simply of doing, and Daniel may yet find it in himself, after the idol of justice has proven false, to take up in some future James novel the actions he once rejected: 'To be seen in the synagogue [is] to proclaim; this is where I stand, these are my people . . . this is what I am' (OS 128). Sonia's sister, Agnes, would have recognized the argument: 'Belief in religion may not influence behaviour. The practice of religion surely should' (OS 277).

Practice without belief is not hypocrisy or superstition – certainly not idolatry. Practice is simply good manners; it is an acceptance of the communal norms above and below the legal written codes at a depth and height far outdistancing mere convention. The law may be an ass, but we do not necessarily choose as a result to live aside from it. I have always been struck that in Canada we have a Federal political party committed to Quebec's separation from the country and refusing with that province to sign on to the 1982 Constitutional proposal while at the same time acting fully within the unwritten constitutional conventions. Manners makyth man and the justice man makes.

The practice of good manners in this sense cannot be finally directed according to a written text alone. To insist on the foundational quality of any such text or theory as final would be idolatrous. What is needed for manners is not a handbook for proper etiquette, but models of behaviour, saints of the moral tradition, known as such by their continuation over time in iconic depictions. The difficulty is that icons can rapidly become idols, a movement well recognized by the earliest cultures.[91] The icon is two-dimensional – it is flat, but is painted in such a way that it draws the eye from below to above and down again, offering the viewer an opening for meditation on the heights and depths of the possibilities it depicts. In James' *Innocent Blood*, for example, mosaics and their iconic significance appear throughout the novel.[92] The icon becomes an idol in its perfidy – when it deceives, that is, when it draws the gaze of the viewer and holds it ('frames' it), convincing the viewer that it, the 'icon', is the reality. By 'framing' the gaze idols direct the gaze not upward to divine possibilities or downward to human limitations (as is the case with the icon), but from left to right, emphasizing particular aspects of the picture and by so focusing the gaze, convincing the viewer that the appearance is reality, that the portrayal is the whole.[93] Thus establishing a delusion of width, limit, and breadth, and by cleverly adapting the technique of perspective it proposes depth where there is mere surface. The computer screen above all gives the impression that it has depth, but this is only an illusion of its range (that it embraces all necessary information) and the supposition that width of information is the same as breadth of analysis. As a result the gaze has no direction for reflection except back on itself. The icon, turned idol, is the water into which Narcissus gazes and cannot escape – it is not the medieval *speculum* (mirror) in which the whole of reality can be caught and understood in its full breadth, albeit 'through a glass darkly'.[94]

Videmus nunc per speculum in aenigmate. An idol, however, cannot afford enigmas. With the growing supremacy of screen capitalism in the late twentieth century, Western culture has grown increasingly flat and stale (although not unprofitable), directing all gazes it can to flat surfaces, television, film, computer screens, billboards. The film's 24 still-life frames per second convince the viewer that there is motion when there is in fact none, and in this deliberate violence to the eye it becomes the best of all media to depict violence and 'voyeuristic' sex. Beauty is indeed in the eye of the beholder and all 'reality TV' is reality. The present alone counts in such a world of pretence, shifting 'relevance' and passing 'popularity'[95] convincing entranced viewers of a past and future without any footings or cover. The world of the flat idol is not the world of the young 'unsophisticated' admirer of a war picture in James' *The Murder Room*. For him it provides a link with the past in a way impossible for those 'sophisticated' figures in the novel who find in the museum and its past only a cover for 'masked' sex. In the world of the flat idol truth is fundamentally in the appearance, what the eye can see, the experiential and experimental. For the idol, all books are dangerous: a book is not flat but deep – it is thick in its many pages, its extensive description, and the possibilities of its interpretation. Idolatrous cultures therefore limit reading, shortening prose to caption-length fillers so that the 'reader' can turn as quickly as possible back to the picture, limiting 'reflections' to 'blinks', and compiling short bursts of narrative so as to leave the impression of length and a good read.[96]

The close ties between idol and icon, between the flat picture that leads the eye astray and the deep book, is hinted at in Daniel's family name, Aaron, and his story in the latter half of *Exodus*. Having led the chosen people out of bondage, their Lord's first requirement (Exodus 20.1ff.) is that they remain free of idols, taking no other gods before him, and avoid all temptations to be bound again to any graven images. Perceiving these command-ments 'in thunderings and lightnings' and fearing them, the people ask for a mediating word, that of Moses, an incarnated human voice (Exodus 20.18–20). Moses then approaches 'the thick darkness where God was' and in that dark silent night the primary commandment is enunciated once more: 'You shall not make gods of silver to be with me, nor shall you make for your-selves gods of gold' (Exodus 20.23), the first co-ordinate warning against iconic representations of the divinity, parallel to the divinity itself (although read temporally, horizontally, from left to right), the second drawing those images down as human gold to human control. In recognition of the creature's structure as a physical entity and its need for physical means to communicate, the Lord then commands an altar to be made to direct the eyes upward to him, on which are to be placed 'burnt offerings', the humble recognition of creatures that they are not their own, and 'peace offerings', the effective communal results of creatures recognizing themselves as equal and as one before him to whom their eyes are raised and who comes to them and blesses them as they do this in memory of him (Exodus 20.24). The altar is not to be sculpted, lest its ends be deemed human ends, and it is not to have steps up to it, lest human beings, trusting themselves, are thereby forgetful of their creaturehood. The patterns for justice are established on this basis and in analogy to the divinity's own six days of creative activity (Exodus 21.1–23.33) to culminate on a seventh day of worship, at the height of which a mediating angelic voice is promised that will put to flight all enemies (Exodus 23.19ff.). Following the enactment of the commands – the establishment of one altar on a diverse communal twelve pillars, the hearing of the read word, and the promise to do all that is spoken – Moses as a representative of the people and recapitulating the earlier 'going up' ascends the mountain, enters a cloud ('of unknowing' as later writers would have it), and on the seventh day is called out before the glory of the Lord 'in the sight of the people', after which he returns into the cloud for the requisite forty days and nights of testing (Exodus 24).

The message with which Moses returns to the people this time parallels the earlier warning against graven images, but seems to contradict it. Six lengthy chapters of instruction follow, detailing precisely the making of the ark of the covenant and associated 'graven' images (Exodus 25 to 30), and culminating in the appointment of those who are to carry out the work, the primeval and archetypical artists, Bezalel, filled 'with the Spirit of God, with ability and intelligence, with knowledge and crafts-manship, to devise artistic designs, . . . to work in every craft', and with him, Oholiab. But they are not appointed alone; they will not replace priests and prophets. They are artists only in so far as they devote their art to the making of images toward the greater glory of God, and with them God has 'given to all able men ability that they may make all that I have commanded you' for 'the holy garments for Aaron the priest and the garments of his sons, *for their service as priests, and the anointing oil and the fragrant incense for the holy place*' (Exodus 31.1–11; emphasis mine). The depth of the biblical text is reiterated in a short section which closes the passage: the commandment to work six days and to rest on the seventh is now offered to sum up the primary work of the community and all within it, namely worship. Moses then comes down from the mountain as he had been described doing twice before, ten chapters and five chapters earlier, delivering the two tablets of the Lord a final third time, only to discover that the people had 'gathered themselves together' and 'up' into a self-made, socially contracted unity before Aaron the priest and had turned their own fashionings into a golden calf to go before them, forgetful of the God above them to which their arts were to point (Exodus 32.1ff.). The task of the artist they give over to utility.[97]

Like his namesake, Daniel Aaron passes by the first piece of evidence he came upon, a flat sheet holding a confession and requiring a reading back into time and not 'before him' in the present. It has fallen from the deep *Book of Common Prayer* that contained it, and he makes no attempt to read it within the tradition of that book, or to interpret it in the context of the perfidy of the 5 November liturgy that attracted his attention for a moment, and then, like all history not relevant to the immediate case at hand, he passed by. He grasps rather the 'body of evidence', the photograph, that turns out at the close of the novel to be unimportant, holding to it as evidence substantially establishing the criminal's guilt. Like a disillusioned worshipper who might eliminate a god by breaking the idol (in substance the god itself), so Daniel proposed to eliminate guilt by removing the idol, for him both the evidence substantiating a particular case of justice and justice itself. His idol is simply an icon rigorously embraced in and for itself alone. The photograph might have served as a genuine icon, had Daniel allowed it to reflect for him Auschwitz, 'the awful necessity of war' (OS 422), and the full implications of the silence of God, but he hears not the negation of that city, only the voices he speaks for it.

The photograph was the murderer's idol as well. It no longer raised his loved ones to him. He does not carry it with him or treasure it in his home – it has become a mere archival object, proving a lost possible heritage in and by itself and demanding the justice of an equal elimination of another's future descendants. But like all idols it so constricts his sight that he fails finally in his attempt to make matters right, perhaps deluded by a literal-minded application of Western Christianity's doctrine of original sin as somehow in the progeneration of physical life itself. He confuses revenge with justice and, like Sonia Clements, believes that justice is the one transcendent, standing above 'our strength, our talent, our memories, our joys, even our capacity to grieve. Why should we let [time] take away the imperative of justice?' (OS 421). Over forty years he had tested the evidence in the wilderness of his own life to be certain he was right. He 'should have kept [his] energies for his poetry', his ability to hear words speak beyond their literal text, but he wasted his life in refusing to face the limitation and inevitability and incomprehension of life and wasted it 'on a useless obsession born of [his] own guilt'. He learns his lesson too late and from the voice of the one he wished to punish. His enemy had no direct, only adopted, heirs. The murderer murdered the innocent as did the one against whom he was to be avenged. 'If you want to act like God, . . . you should first ensure that you have the wisdom and knowledge of God.' When the idol collapses, the one who loves it does so as well. None can rejoice in watching the result, not even if the one suffering is one's own potential killer:

> [She] knew that [he] didn't need to ask if this was the truth. . . . For a moment she saw him physically crumble. . . . [E]verything that was alive in him drained away in front of her eyes. . . . [S]lowly and painfully he forced himself to stand upright, . . . turned and made for the door, . . . [went] through the hall and into the night. . . . (OS 422–3)

The woman described here is the one he wished to kill and her action is significant. She reaches out in love to him and can acknowledge: 'I am myself at last. I have something worth giving [another].' Daniel can only utter: 'Let him be. Let him be.' Daniel's words are in imitation of the divine 'Fiat' (The 'Let there be' of Genesis 1, a *fiat sola!*) projected outward on another. It is his attempt to speak the creative word, his unwillingness even in catastrophe to recognize the human response required of it in silence. The result is described by James as a small coterie of those who remain parting from one another's fleeting embrace in 'this sodden wasteland [and] waited in silence. . . . The silence was absolute' (OS 423).

And yet, the absolute silence here is a prospect of hope. It is the silence of the Blessed Virgin who waits in absolute humility, in the nothingness of her own voice, allowing the Word to create new heavens and a new earth in her *ex nihilo*. The fiat that is required is that of Mary's words in Luke 1.38: *Fiat mihi secun-*

dum verbum tuum, Let it be done to me according to your word, a *fiat* standing not alone (*sola,* the act of a god), but open to the action of another. If the silence is absolute, it may well, indeed, be that in the disintegration of the murderer himself, and his walk into the night, a redemptive word might yet be heard. 'Between the stirrup and the ground', after all, there is many a soul lost *and* many a soul found. Daniel waits with the others in what we are told is an absolute silence, in which no human voices demand their own hearing. In this silence he too has hope; it is the same silence in which, at the end of the novel, he walks with Kate. The idols seem no longer to have power over him, certainly not in the way they do for Karen Suretees (a pun on 'certain'?), the deceit-ful journalist in *Death in Holy Orders,* who continues to need a 'real' consecrated sacrament (even though she does not believe in that reality) to bribe her way into a Black Mass so as to report the 'truth'. 'If you were an investigative journalist you took the job seriously, conscientious even in deceit' (DHO 336). What she fails to recognize is that the only importance of her work lies in its use as wrapping for other more wholesome produce and its chance spurring of a real human memory and genuine evidence (DHO 102).

There is an interesting parallel to Daniel's situation with Meg's in *Devices and Desires.* She too has evidence to convict a killer, but considering good manners first and abstract justice second, she struggles with the dilemma whether to speak directly to the murderer (for whom she seeks 'redemption'), or not. She seeks advice from a priest with a question of conscience. Conscience, the priest tells her, is the voice of God. For Meg, God is in fact silent, and she recognizes the way in which this silencing has occurred and confronts it: 'But how can we be sure that what we're hearing isn't our own voice, our own subconscious desires? The message we listen for so carefully must be mediated through our own experience, our personality, our heredity, our inner needs. Can we ever break free of the devices and desires of our own hearts? Might not our conscience be telling us what we most want to hear?' For the priest this is not the case. 'I haven't found it so,' he replies: 'Conscience has usually directed me against my own desires.' As such, conscience is not the human voice speaking, but silent and listening. But surely, she asks: '[A]ny human decision has to take account of the probable consequences; that is surely what decision means. How can we separate cause from effect?' (DD 475–6). The response is a simple suggestion that she 'leave the consequences to God', that it is not the place of individual human beings to judge the finality of the final cause, to know the ultimate truth toward which an action or an event was created. Not surprisingly, '[s]he wanted to say, "Even if we're not sure any longer if he exists? Even if that seems only another way of evading the personal responsibility which you have just told me we can't and shouldn't evade?"' (DD 377). The answer we are given to suppose is 'Yes.'

Loss and justice: the case of Kate Miskin

Unlike Daniel Aaron, Kate Miskin is caught in silence without a past to reject. She was not raised in a religious family and what remains to her of religious language is mere snatches. Caring for an ageing and increasingly confused grandmother (who loved crime films (CJ 175)), one need not overpress her name to point to her lack of kin. She needs to 'picture' the activity in an early morning church service and she is deeply confused by a woman who makes a confession but is not a regular member of the congregation. '[W]hat had brought her into the church to seek [the priest's] advice, to make her confession, to receive absolution? Absolution from what?' (CJ 303). The heritage that overburdened Daniel is not hers; she moves from *Original Sin* to *A Certain Justice*, taking on as an associate Piers Tarrant, the theologian atheist. Incapable of understanding religious life and having nowhere else to gain a horizon to live by, she, like Daniel, chooses the law and justice. 'You had at some point to say: This is what I choose to believe. To this I shall give my loyalty. With her it had been the police service.'

Unlike Daniel, however, Kate grants no finality to justice – she does not idolize it. Like her senior, Dalgliesh, she knows that justice is a 'large word' and would rather speak of the 'cause of truth' (MR 241). She attends to evidence and will not allow a court of law higher than that of evidence, particularly that of the priest and the confessional. She fears the evidence the priest may have received in the confessional can be destroyed, and when assured that the priest will not do so, but may not give it, she can only think that '[h]e must give it to us. He can't conceal evidence. There must be a way of compelling him to hand it over' (CJ 304). Nevertheless, she knows that her system is not final. 'You didn't need to go to Oxford to learn [the principles in which she believed]. But what did it say when confronted with a tortured and murdered child, or with that body lying like a butchered animal, the throat cut to the bone?' And she is willing to admit that there may be a religious answer: 'If so, could it really be found in this dim, incense-laden air?' (CJ 305). It is a question but it is an open one.

She is open as well in lesser matters. She looks beyond the particulars of evidence to the system at large and is willing to accept its limitations. Speaking to a kidnap victim in *A Certain Justice* she implicitly admits that the perpetrator of the central crime may never be caught. 'Suspicion isn't enough. We have to have evidence, evidence that will stand up in court. The police don't prosecute. That decision is for the Director of Public Prosecutions and she needs to be satisfied that there is at least a fifty per cent chance of getting a conviction' (CJ 381–2). The victim, whose murdered mother was a clever lawyer who cared little about the guilt or innocence of her clients, knows that even if prosecuted, the criminal can be set free, and Kate accepts the complaint: 'It is a funny system, but it is the best we have. We can never expect perfect justice. We have a system that sometimes lets the guilty go free so that the innocent can live in safety under the law' (CJ 383).

Kate has continued to learn from Dalgliesh. She knows that justice is the new reduced form of 'manners', and, like Dalgliesh in *Devices and Desires*, when others reject a morality as 'absolute

. . . independent of time or circumstance', perhaps would be 'content that there is such a thing, that Mrs Dennison's natural repugnance tell[s] us something about the morality of the act [of conceiving a child deliberately in order to kill it to make use of its tissue]' (DD 76). The difficulty is that the socially mannered form reflective of Mrs Dennison's morality is collapsing as well. *A Certain Justice* considers the collapse of this system, in which the lawyers operate for profit and pride and a legal defender is the criminal. Kate knows it is collapsing and she acknowledges the fact. The system is flawed and she is limited – 'fallen' or 'sinful' might have been adjectives available to her could she understand them. Murderers may go free, new Cains justifying themselves in their endeavour to be like God, extending the initial desire of Adam and Eve. The psychopath is freed to kill again, but even if he were not, Kate knows that the existence of such a person is the problem: 'psychopath, that convenient word devised to explain, categorize, and define in statute law the unintelligible mystery of human evil'.[98]

Although constraining the impact of the term 'evil' to some extent with the adjective 'human' in this comment, Kate nevertheless is willing to admit its unintelligible mystery, explainable in a number of ways, perhaps even in a religious system.

[W]ere we any closer to knowing the answer? Perhaps for some people it lay in the incense-laden air of St James's Church. If so, it had never been open to her. But the altar-table was, after all, only an ordinary table covered with gorgeous cloth. The candles were wax candles. The statue of the Virgin had been made by human hands, painted, bought, fixed in place. Under his cassock and his robes Father Presteign was only a man. Was what he offered part of some complicated system of belief, richly adorned, embellished with ritual and music, pictures and stained glass, designed, like the law itself, to bring men and women to the comforting illusion that there was an ultimate justice and that they had a choice? (CJ 383)

To her surprise Kate discovers that choice is indeed possible. Her past was the same as that of the psychopath; they had grown up in the same neighbourhood. His victim who loved him argued that he never had a chance and Kate argued that he did. She now transfers the argument to herself and understands her chance as choice. She is, in a sense, the new Eve, choosing not to be like a god, but to accept life in a fallen world and to live in the 'broken middle'.[99] She, unlike the psychopath, can respond. She recognizes the 'givenness' of her life, however little is given – she looks after her grandmother; the psychopath kills his aunt – and in that recognition grasps her ability to respond, her response-ability and thereby her freedom. The murder victim, responsible in large part for her own death although not grasping the implications of responsibility, once stated: '[W]hen people say there's nothing to choose, they mean that they want to avoid the responsibility of choosing' (CJ 61). Kate could have agreed and been able to maintain and reconstruct the iconic dimension of her view of justice: 'You're a policeman. You have to believe in free will' (CJ 263).

For Kate the 'have to' no longer defines an obligatory force as it does for Daniel. In her open view of justice and her acknowledgement of her past, she enacts what the Christian tradition refers to as confession (a theme we will take up in the final chapter) and knows the reality of choice and responsibility in her life and that of others. She is freed from any falsifying idol and her loss of a religious life she never had or understood is repaired and open for renewal, as she with Daniel at the close of *Original Sin* walks in a silence, neither any longer isolated in their individual solitudes (the silence of God's voice overpowered by human cacophonies endeavouring to create) but now knowing a silence offering open possibilities for them to speak humbly and pro-creatively (the subjective silence of God establishing freedom for humanity).

The historical past and justice in *An Instance of the Fingerpost*

In the work of Ian Pears (James' next door Oxford neighbour) the refusal to acknowledge the past consistently serves as a sign (fingerpost), pointing to a character trait that both idolizes justice and seeks to avoid it by reconstructing remembered events into a less personally offensive narrative. Since the search for the murderer and justice always entails a search into past events, the skills a detective requires inevitably coalesce with those of the historian, searching the archives and studying artefacts. Individuals seeking to avoid judgement must inevitably make use of the same skills in their reconstruction of the historical narrative.

An Instance of the Fingerpost is the story of a murder in late seventeenth-century Oxford, told from the perspective of four different narrators, offering the reader a choice of four possible conclusions regarding the events and requiring a judgement on the historical case presented (it includes real historical figures and fictional characters) and the nature of historical truth itself. As the adage from Cicero's *De Oratore* that opens the book has it: 'Historia vero testis temporum, lux veritatis, vita memoriae, magistra vitae.' History truly is the witness of the times, the light of truth, the life of memory, the teacher of life (translation mine). The search for the murderer, as we have been here arguing, establishes history and can be arrived at only through history. Only from witnesses of the times in which an event occurred can the light of truth be established. The chiastic formation (A: life B: memory, A: teacher B: life) of Cicero's rhetoric links our instruction in how to live (manners) with the vitality of memories of those manners. We live by the truth, that is, by testimonies transmitted through memories, and we are taught by the resulting tradition.

All the characters in Pears' novel are seeking to tell the truth of past events so as to justify their own place in those events and thereby to make justice as they make history. The difficulty is that they do so on a seventeenth-century Baconian model of truth, the model of truth of their own times, the one they bequeathed to the modern age, a model of inductive, experimental science, and, tragically, idolatrous. Each of the sections of the novel, introducing the differing narratives, opens with a quotation from Francis Bacon's *Novum Organum*. The first opens with 'A Question of Precedence: "There are Idols which we call Idols of the Market. For Men associate by Discourse, and a false and improper Imposition of Words strangely possesses the Understanding, for Words absolutely force the Understanding, and put all Things into Confusion." Francis Bacon, Novum Organum Scientarum, Section I, Aphorism VI' (IF 1). The idols of the marketplace, of the flat silver screen, are those which have precedence, that is, those which are popular and command the attention of prospective consumers, striving to imitate and incorporate the lives before them. The idols of the marketplace impose words improperly, strangely possessing and absolutely forcing an enslaved understanding so that all life is confused. Such idols engage, according to Bacon, 'The Great Trust' in particulars, in what we call ideas, forged in the Platonic cave of separated solipsistic creatures and corrupting the light of nature, itself unmindful, the reader is given to believe, of the light of truth, the memory and teacher of life.[100] How aware Bacon was of his foresight with respect to the new organum he was developing is difficult to say, but the epigram with which Pears chooses to open the third section of his novel points to new idols that arise naturally from the great trust, reinstantiating the idols of the marketplace, precedence, and popularity in compliance with a world of theatre, entertainment now growing directly on a marketplace economy, its discourse already in Bacon's time reinterpreting all earlier searches for wisdom as fictitious stage plays.[101]

On the Baconian model the means to escape the resulting dilemma requires a search for evidence provided by 'An Instance of the Fingerpost: "When in a Search of any Nature the Understanding stands suspended, then Instances of the Fingerpost shew the true and inviolable Way in which the Question is to be decided. These Instances afford great Light, so that the Course of the Investigation will sometimes be terminated by them. Sometimes, indeed, these Instances are found amongst that Evidence already set down." Francis Bacon, Novum Organum Scientarum, Section XXXVI, Aphorism XXI' (IF 529). But what Bacon, the characters in the novel, and postmodern readers of the novel enamoured with theories of the social construction of truth and cultural diversity fail to grasp is that the programmatic instances of fingerposts point not to great light but to an unexpected termination. The difficulty is that on the Baconian model of truth, pointing, it is supposed, into the future, the male experimenter establishes a history rooted in her or his own history and with this novel and idolatrous narrative replaces the human, mannered tradition, the life of memory, the mistress-teacher (*magistra*) of life with his or her own newly constructed self.

As the argument unfolds in these selections, Bacon proves himself the prophet of a coming idolatry, based on the programme he proposed and the idols he is seeking to avoid. Behind it lurked a problematic understanding of truth as evident in nature. According to Aristotle the truths of nature could be understood according to four causes: material, effective, formal, and final. The pen with which I am writing can be known by the materials that make it up (plastic, metal, ink), by the effective process out of which it came (company and local stationer), by its form (cylindrical shape descending to a sharpened point), and by the purpose for which it was made, its end: namely, to write. In the Aristotelian system taken up in Christian theology the primary cause was the final, but that final cause was never understood simply as pragmatic. As all things were made through God, so the truth of all things could be known only finally in light of the purposes of God. My pen, we might propose, is a true pen since it writes. But in this argument the truth of my pen is not that it writes, but that it serves as an example to explain an Aristotelian concept of truth. It is a true pen because it writes and it is a true pen because it serves as an example. Under the aspect of eternity its end was not only to write. And who is to say that its exemplary function is its final end? It may be that this pen will be passed on some time to a friend who will use it to compile the formulae to heal some debilitating disease. Aware of this it behoves me to conservative action, to protect the pen and to respect it as a past given over to my care for the future.

When the final cause is given primacy in the search for truth and that search remains open under the sight of a transcendent divinity, two things happen. First, as we have already noted in our earlier comment on Augustine and interpretation, there can be growth in truth, a hierarchy of truths, indeed, many truths. Second, the search is future-focused and the future is open into the divine meaning itself. On the Baconian model of the truth of inductive science (if established as a sovereign model), the search for truth is always back in time, a search for origins, an engagement with understanding material and effective causes, a concern with the final cause solely for pragmatic results, and history as scientific, but backward. The future as a result is limited by the limitations of the creature, and the apprehensions of traditional wisdom are replaced by the findings and narratives of the historical-critical method, themselves obscuring origins in their very insistence that they have comprehended them. The many truths that now arise, dependent on the many and varying narratives constructed, are no longer the manifold hierarchical and open truths of the older method, but the diverse and relative truths locked in an antiquarian past, open to reflection by the present as museum objects, increasingly judged as aesthetic or capital commodities.

Nor need any origins be acknowledged or confessed. This is no longer the history of Cicero, a genre within the study of ethics and 'offices', that is, moral obligations. Modern Prosperos have no need to acknowledge things of darkness as their own. They have after all 'come upon' them; the evidence is of the past, of an era long decayed before the progressive present. Thus, in *An Instance of the Fingerpost* all four characters rewrite their testimonies of the past, placing all hope in that their individual narrations will each serve as the final narrative bequeathed to and accepted by future generations. In this they seek their self-justification, although recognizing as they do so the tenuousness of their attempt. Marco da Cola, the first narrator, claims his final act is a small act of corporal mercy at one remove, but, knowing his own conspiratorial personality, he cannot trust that others are any different from himself and in this humility, perhaps, will eventually have the opportunity for redemption:

> I gave him a pound, and asked him to see to Mrs Blundy's funeral, so that she might avoid a pauper's grave. . . .
>
> He agreed to take care of it for me. I do not know whether he kept his word. (IF 195)

For the second narrator, Jack Prescott, even so narrow an opening is firmly closed in the assurance that his espionage is justified by his political and worldly success. Those whom the Lord loves, he blesses, according to his sovereign will, now expressed through his elect, who have no need in a divinely predestined and closed world to seek for grace any longer:

> In effect, there ends my story. . . .
>
> I have done much in my life which I regret and, if I had the opportunity, there is much I would do differently. But my task was all important, and I feel reassured that I am acquitted of any serious offence. The Lord has been good, and though no man deserves it, my salvation has been no injustice. I would not have so much, and such a tranquillity of mind, had I not been blessed by His Merciful Providence. In Him I place all my trust, and have endeavoured only to serve as best I can. My vindication is my assurance of His favour. (IF 372)

The inevitable loss that results from Prescott's form of theological certitude is experienced by the third narrator, John Wallis. Like Prescott, and the fourth writer Anthony Wood, he is convinced that his actions have saved his country from an inevitable catastrophe. 'That fact, and that alone, more than justifies all I did,' he asserts. Any failures are the result of others' trickery, and any sufferings he 'imposed on others' were 'motivated solely by my desire for justice and [I] always thought this excuse enough'. And like Prescott, Wallis supports his narrative with a theological explanation: 'All is known to the highest Judge of all and to Him I must entrust my soul, knowing that I have served Him to the best of my ability in all my acts.' The difficulty, however, is that for Wallis, the modern man, theological certitude has lost its hold and that even the opening provided in a hope for salvation which may remain for da Cola is lost in Wallis' replacement of it in another belief system that denies the possibility of transcendental justice:

> But often now, late at night when I lie sleepless in my bed once more, or when I am deep in the frustration of prayers which no longer come, I fear my only hope of salvation is that His mercy will prove greater than was mine.
> I no longer believe it will. (IF 527)

Once belief in a hope transcending self-narration is suspended by dis-belief, there is no way to turn, it appears, but to the evidence of this world that alone remains. For Anthony Wood, who utters a final word in *An Instance of the Fingerpost*, the pearl of great price lies in the evidence or the 'continued obscurity' of a flat piece of paper. The last word is that of an antiquarian who recognizes the fragility of fingerposts and their obscure directives, including the language of incarnation, forgiveness, and grace. Preserved as a symbolic means for understanding the limitations of life, in one sense that language is silenced, brought down to earth by a Feuerbachian turn and incorporated in the fragility of matter alone. As in Eliot's *Middlemarch*, the reader is here invited to revisit 'the number who lived faithfully a hidden life, and rest in unvisited tombs':

> [H]ow paltry all this is to a man who has seen such marvels, and felt such grace, as I have seen and felt. I do believe and

know that I have seen and heard and touched the incarnate God. Quietly, out of sight of mankind, divine forgiveness descends again, and we are so blind we do not even realise what inexhaustible patience and love is ours. Thus it happened, and has happened in every generation and will happen again in every generation to come, that a beggar, a cripple, a child, a madman, a criminal or a woman is born Lord of us all in entire obscurity, and is spurned and ignored and killed by us to expiate our sins. And I am commanded to tell no one, and I will keep that one commandment.

This is the truth, the one and only truth, manifest, complete and perfect. Besides it, what importance have the dogma of priests, the strength of kings, the rigour of scholars or the ingenuity of our men of science? (IF 691)

The passage deserves close analysis in light of what we have seen in Kate Miskin's insights. Wood too recognizes the paltriness of human existence, but he does not share it. He is the one who has seen the marvels and felt the grace. He is the one who understands the way to interpret divine forgiveness. He knows it is operative in silence ('quietly'), but he will not allow a silence to remain as silence into which a new creative word might speak. Wood speaks. He and he alone (except for the readers who identify with him and stand alongside him in his superiority) designates the rest of humanity as blind to the truth, the truth that divine forgiveness is not transcendent, but *'is ours'*, humanity's 'patience and love', and is 'inexhaustible', enduring no limit as it progresses into 'every generation to come'. It may well be that the lowly, the entirely obscure, the abused, are 'Lord of us all'. The unnoted ironic turn is that their advocate, the one who has seen and felt such grace, who knows the absolute truth, 'the one and only truth, manifest, complete and perfect', stands well above all these lords and the rest of benighted humanity, maintaining as his own private possession the gnostic messianic secret, obedient to the limited commandment of a single Gospel 'to tell no one' so as to control truth and require justice above all human manners: 'the dogma of priests, the strength of kings, the rigour of scholars or the ingenuity of our men of science'. The silence of God is the silence of graced humanity, refusing to acknowledge the gift it received as another's or itself as anything other than divine. The antiquarian, preserving the past in the museum of his own private domain, points resolutely to humanity's unattained and perhaps unattainable future possibilities so as to avoid any investigation of human witnesses, to misdirect their testimonies, and to remain ever the authoritative teacher, never the humble student whom he will be pleased to counsel to contemplate her own ignorance.[102]

For Wood the antiquarian the truth remains transcendent, not to him, but in him; it substantiates his own transcendence. What he fails to recognize in all his disquisitions on the nature of history is what Kate Miskin knows well: that truth is formulated first within a communal context and is thus upheld not as a demand for the intellect but as moral practice required by the eighth commandment: not bearing false witness.[103] Truth is established on reliable testimonies regarding past events and mediated in those events. It is apprehended only in a human tradition, not outside of it. This Kate understands full well in her role as a detective and she applies it in her search for self-understanding. In *The Murder Room* the past as a museum collection 'oppressed her from the moment of her first entry. There was something alien to her spirit about its careful recon-struction of the past.' She knew that the human story at large or any part of that story could not be so simply controlled and she knew it in light of her own experience. 'For years she had tried to throw off her own history and she resented and was half afraid of the clarity and the awful inevitability with which it was now returning month by month.' In her attempt to overcome her personal history, she held to the principle that '[t]he past was dead, finished with, unalterable. Nothing about it could be com-pensated for and surely nothing fully understood.' Past life as a whole could have no meaning, she contended. 'Some of these people were buried in quicklime and some in churchyards, but they might just as well have been dumped together in a common grave for all that mattered now.' What mattered was the present. The question to be asked is '*How can I live safely except in this present moment, the moment which, even as I measure it, becomes the past?*' (MR 252; emphasis original). But the force of the question as an assertion reminds her of an incident somewhat earlier in which it was evident to her that her past was not past. After visiting one of the witnesses she discovered herself responding in anger. 'She had spent years and energy putting the past behind her: her illegitimacy, the acceptance that she would now never know the name of her father, the life in the city tower block with her disgruntled grandmother, the smell, the noise, the all-pervading hopelessness.' But she is 'essentially honest [and] she recognised [her reaction] with some shame: it was class-resentment' in spite of her intentions. The past was still with her (MR 198). Later, reflecting on this experience, the same 'uneasy conviction . . . returned. She couldn't safely confront those early years or nullify their power by being a traitor to her past' (MR 252).

It is not a question of Kate confronting her past; it may be too complex to engage it in full or perhaps too traumatic for her to face, but she will not, by some psychotherapeutic technique, eliminate its hold on her. She will continue to pass it on as a *traditio* (a thing handed on); she will not play the role of *traditor*, a traitor – the one who hands over the tradition to the enemy so as to live another tradition. In this recognition and acknowledgement lie the seeds of rebirth – to know the truth and to be thereby set free, to allow the past to speak in the silence and to allow the opportunity for acknowledgement, confession where acknowledged as appropriate, and reform. The world is not closed. There is Christian opportunity, the possibility of new life beyond the supposed necessities of social and biological forms and yet fully within them, their destructive reality (one's unity with the murderers) and openness to justice and the good.

4

Remembrance, thanksgiving, and final release: How Freud got it wrong

The final scene of James' *Death in Holy Orders* offers a good beginning to close this series of essays. The murderer is known, a certain justice is fulfilled, and we are left to ponder the nature of the death in holy orders by facing once more a papyrus fragment, up to this point a supposedly 'false' clue to the mystery. Appropriately known as the Anselm papyrus, '[i]t's reputed to be an order, ostensibly signed by Pontius Pilate to the captain of the guard ordering the removal of the crucified body of a political troublemaker' (DHO 242) and it may well be authentic:

> Father Martin had finished preparing his fireplace. Now he took from the canvas bag a sheet of newspaper and bunched it into the hollow. Then he laid the Anselm papyrus above it and, crouching, struck a match. The paper caught fire immediately and it seemed that the flames leapt at the papyrus as if it were prey. The heat for a moment was intense and he stepped back. He saw that Raphael had come beside him and was silently watching. Then he said,
> 'What are you burning, Father?'
> 'Some writing which has already tempted someone to sin and may tempt others. It's time for it to go.'

There was a silence, then Raphael said, 'I shan't make a bad priest, Father.'

Father Martin, the least demonstrative of men, laid a hand briefly on his shoulder and said, 'No, my son. I think you may make a good one.'

Then they watched together in silence as the fire died down and the last frail wisp of white smoke drifted over the sea. (DHO 387)

There are a number of things worthy of note here, the first of which is the silence in which the episode takes place. Raphael silently watches and after an enigmatic answer to his simple question there is silence once more, only to be broken by a response, before the final silence of the narrative's end. In fact the last silence marks the end of two narratives, that of the story of Raphael and Father Martin as told in the novel, *Death in Holy Orders*, and that of another narrative regarding the Christian tradition in which both men will continue to live. Father Martin is involved in a 'cover-up'. A document exists that, if authentic, proves the Christian tradition's teaching regarding the empty tomb false. It was not a miraculous event, after all. If the Anselm document is to be believed, Jesus' body was removed by perfectly ordinary means to rest in an 'unvisited tomb,' hidden from them as a centre for any future 'political troublemakers'. Whoever killed Jesus managed the near-perfect murder, eliminating not only his life, but the body as well, and now Father Martin, conspiring with the murderers, perfects their act and eliminates the only piece of evidence that there ever was such a person. 'You must have a body' before a charge can be laid, but there is no body or any evidence of a body. There can be no trial; no one can be charged as guilty.

A tradition lost

There is a further silencing as well. Father Martin's act silences the tradition he is committed to save. He, the astute Raphael, and the reader know the content of the burning papyrus. In the world beyond the novel's close, like the world after Auschwitz and Nagasaki, any faith accorded an empty tomb will dwell in doubt. Having heard of one, albeit fictionalized text, modern readers will speculate that there may have been other papyri no longer extant. Like Dalgliesh they are committed to the importance of the evidence and cannot set it aside or explain it away. Dalgliesh once suggested that we must seek the truth 'however unwelcome it may be when we find it' (DHO 249). Even possible evidence requires explanation. What *might* have been, might have *been*. Absence, silence proves its own undoing for modern minds and thus offers a route to salvation. This Father Martin understands. The Anselm papyrus is, after all, Anselmian. The reader was introduced to a priest's fireplace early in the novel over which hung the motto of the school and its namesake – 'credo ut intellegam' (I believe so that I might understand) (DHO 32) – and at the close of the book another priest prepares the fire to destroy an idol, itself destructive of truth, whether arrived at by faith or understanding. The modern reader, shocked at the permanent removal of such evidence, needs to be reminded of the photograph at the close of *Original Sin*, the body in the open tomb as it were, that 'didn't matter any more'. Hidden, secret, 'framed' (DHO 247), the papyrus had forced attention on the fact and not beyond it. The question it raised was the question of its own authenticity, not the reality of that to which it pointed. As such, Father Martin argues, it is better off gone so that faith may continue to seek understanding.

Dalgliesh was once told that his job as a detective concerned with justice was 'a searching for truth', but was then warned about the reality of the endeavour: 'You never get the whole truth of course. How could you? You're a very clever man but what you do doesn't result in justice. There's the justice of men and the justice of God.' With these words, Father Martin foretold his own final act in the novel. He will conspire with the murder of Jesus, removing all possible proof of his life on earth and silencing the very God he believed in. There is no body in the tomb, and there is no evidence of the body. If the tomb were not empty (to turn the Pauline words slightly) our faith is in vain. Carbon dating will not stop controversy over the papyrus. The historical-critical method is of little use in establishing a documentary authority. Dalgliesh wonders however: 'if the papyrus were examined and it were possible to know with almost complete certainty that it was genuine, would that make a difference to your faith?' The answer is negative. 'Father Martin smiled' as we have seen Meg Denison do on gaining her insight on the relationship between truth and love. 'He said: My son, for one who every hour of his life has the assurance of the living presence of Christ, why should I worry about what happened to earthly bones?' (DHO 249) After all, divinity itself chose an emptying of itself into death. Its very humble silence is the content of it and its followers' lives. The Victim of Father Martin's and the soon-to-be Father Raphael's daily sacrifice is the victim who will not victimize, the Word, open to being not heard.

Father Martin (his name reminiscent of Martin Luther whose own fire in 1520 burned a Pope's Bull) is not therefore burning the papyrus as Daniel Aaron attempted to destroy evidence. The evidence of the tradition's life is clear for him in the consecrated Eucharist, a presence so real that even an unbelieving journalist would accept it only in its authentic form, and a troubled believer, involved in its desecration, took his life. In any event, all other evidences of the tradition in which Father Martin believes have already gone. He has no reason to commit an historical felony to protect the faith, already under attack from within. St Anselm's theological college is slipping into the sea and what remains will be sold or transformed into its opposite. It may soon mark the landscape something in the way the ruined Benedictine abbey in *Devices and Desires* does, 'the decaying symbol of a very different power' than that of a nuclear plant (DD 85). 'The sea is advancing rapidly along the coast' (DHO 117), we are told, and throughout the novel the reader is reminded of one overarching symbol of its end, that of the Judgement, portrayed in a painting of Doom. 'The Church they serve is dying', says one character, a murderer (DHO 254). The adoptive father of the dead seminarian takes it as incontestable that the Church has been dead since the mid-1980s (DHO 18), and his words are supported in a semi-comic scene concerning the Creed in which Sir Alred, a far-diminished form of his namesake, the great Cistercian of Rievaulx, is surprised that there are more creeds than one, has reservations regarding its teaching, and can't think why they don't 'bring it up to date. . . . We don't look to the fourth century for our understanding of medicine or science.' To his listener, Dalgliesh, it appears that he 'had it in mind to write one' (DHO 19–20). Lay ignorance of this sort aside, the faith struggles to maintain itself against the leadership called to serve it. Archdiaconal direction is concerned only with pragmatic relevance and cash. The study of biblical languages is to be cast aside in favour of sociological analysis (DHO 127).

> 'St. Anselm's has become irrelevant to the new age.' [says the Archdeacon]
>   Father Sebastian said, 'What is it that you want? A Church without mystery, stripped of that learning, tolerance and dignity that were the virtues of Anglicanism? A Church without humility in the face of the ineffable mystery and love of Almighty God? Services with banal hymns, a debased liturgy and the Eucharist conducted as if it were a parish bean-feast? A Church for Cool Britannia?'

The two walk 'in silence along the north wall', that area of darkness in a church overcome daily by the reading of the Word. For the Archdeacon there is silence simply because the response, a reiteration of his own voice, seems obvious. For Father Sebastian, however, the question is more complex; all that he knows as good is dying and speaks no longer. In this silence 'Father Sebastian suddenly halted. He said, "There's someone here with us. We're not alone"' (DHO 128).

Father Sebastian's words speak beyond their simple intent in a novel that depends for some of its entertainment on suspense. In the silence resulting from the Archdeacon's expressed plans for the future, the older priest recognizes his own inability to maintain his world, but does not console himself with a cynical or nostalgic charm 'of failure and disappointment',[104] either of which idolize the dying remnants of a lost tradition. One might compare and contrast his situation with that of characters in James' *The Murder Room*, in which some hope that '[t]he revitalizing of the museum [will] provide an interest which [will] replace and redeem the dead undistinguished years' (MR 30) against those who, like the Archdeacon, insist that 'we can't go on living in the past and the present political set-up is on our side' (MR 34), or, faced with death, pursue their curatorial functions as a form of 'accidie, [a] lethargy of the spirit' (MR 54) and write history 'as a justification for [their individual] life' (MR 53). 'Memory', we are told, 'is best held at bay by action' (DHO 154).

> '*These fragments I have shored up against my ruins*. Was this the reason? Was it he himself that he needed to immortalize? Was the museum, founded by him and in his name, his personal alms to oblivion? Perhaps this was the attraction of all museums. . . . In making memorials not only to the famous but to the legions of the anonymous dead, were we hoping to ensure our own vicarious immortality?' (MR 26)

The struggle to preserve past idolatries fails in the presence of greater, more pretentious ones: 'Museums honour the past in an age which worships modernity almost as much as it does money and celebrity. It's hardly surprising that museums are in difficulties' (MR 203). The Archdeacon has simply traded one idol for another. In his desire to meet the needs of the modern world he has committed himself to its voice. He cannot trust with his Catholic co-believers that the succession of the apostolic word will continue by daily honouring a living past in a simple Eucharistic act of memory. Like Venetia Aldridge in *A Certain Justice* he appears always trying 'to discipline that part of [his] mind which [he] suspected could be seduced by tradition or history' (CJ 3). For Father Martin it is otherwise. He can trust the proclamation to an orphaned child, Raphael, and to those Mary-like characters like Tully Clutton in *The Murder Room* for whom the voice of God is silent, but is willing to 'live in the past. Not my own past, that's very unexciting and ordinary – but the past of all the people who have been Londoners before me. I never walk there alone, no one can' (MR 58).

The orphaned child is one of the clearest indicators of a lost tradition, but before taking up that theme, we must review the way in which a lost tradition, its voice silenced, continues. For this we turn to Colin Dexter's last book in the Morse series, *The Remorseful Day*.[105] In this novel death becomes Morse's immediate neighbour. Again a Housman poem, from which the title is taken, seems initially to tell the tale: 'How hopeless under ground/ Falls the remorseful day' (*More Poems* (1936), XVI). But a 'remorseful day' linked with a chief character, Morse, offers something more than hopelessness. Remorse is the first step to repentance and confession and thereby to the beginning of a new life. It is possible, even in Morse's remembrances of scattered bits from earlier hymns and artefacts from a culture now dying, that there could lurk the new beginnings and Morse could be remade (re-morsed) even in these nostalgic elements of remorse. To sorrow for a past time is to recognize a better one.

Following a negative medical report regarding his health at the Radcliffe Infirmary and needing a drink before licensed opening hours, Morse turns out of the front door and finds himself, less than a block away, at the Oratorian Roman Catholic Church of St Aloysius. As Oxford tourists will know, he needed to deliberately turn in through the entrance and a simple courtyard, hidden as the church is from the main street. A lover of great music, but not particularly interested in architecture, Morse has no reason to attend to this building. '[H]e'd seldom paid attention to [it] before, although he must have walked past it so many, many times. . . . and the reason why he now checked his step remains inexplicable.'

He entered and looked around him: all surprisingly large and imposing, with a faint, seductive smell of incense, and statues of assorted saints around him, with tiers of candles lit beside their sandalled, holy feet.

A youngish woman had come in behind him. . . . She dipped her right hand into the little font of blessed water there, then crossed herself and knelt in one of the rear pews. Morse envied her, for she looked so much at home there. . . . As she left, Morse could see some of the contents of the carrier bag: a Hovis loaf and a bottle of red plonk.

Bread and wine.

The door clicked to behind her, and Morse stepped over to meet St Anthony, . . . clearly capable of performing quite incredible miracles for those who almost had sufficient faith. Morse picked up a candle from the box there and stuck it in an empty socket on the top row. At which point (it appeared) most worshippers would have prayed fervently for a miracle. But Morse wasn't at all sure what miracle he wanted.

The candles cost him two pounds, the cost of a 'whole pint'. And a miracle occurs: 'As he walked down St Giles', the man who had virtually no faith in the Almighty and even less in miracles noted that the past few minutes had slipped by quickly, . . . that [i]t was now just after 11 a.m.' and that the front door of the Bird and Baby pub 'was open' (RD 171–2). Miracles, then, do happen, simple though they be for a man who on entering hospital realizes that he must write 'None' on the form asking his religious affiliation (RD 344). Nevertheless, Morse stands above most of his colleagues. He recognizes the allusion in the words of a young constable as a 'man under authority' (RD 324), noting ironically that some are fittingly more acquainted with Scripture than the more learned, secularized suspect (RD 327).

Whatever his religious shortcomings, Morse remains, we are assured, 'surrounded by a great cloud of witnesses' (Hebrews 12.1; RD 256), his dying father among them. He has a parentage from which he has gained insights and in this last novel he gains an identity: his associate and his readers finally learn his given name and with this knowledge have a hint of the firm religious background of his upbringing. He is not an orphan. He has a heritage, not forgotten, to which, at the close of his life, he appears to commit himself, setting aside all self-interest, including that of final redemption:[106]

> Morse was fully conscious of what was going on around him. He felt fairly sure that he was dying, and pretended to himself that he would face death with at least some degree of dignity, if not with equanimity. He had been seated beside his old father when he'd died, and heard him reciting the Lord's Prayer, as if it were some sort of insurance policy. And Morse wondered whether his own self-interest might possibly be served by following suit. But if by any freak of chance there was an Almighty, well, He'd understand anyway; and since, in Morse's view, there wasn't, he'd be wasting his really (at this time) rather precious breath.

All hope is gone, and yet there is a glimmer, perhaps even more in the silence into which Morse, a representative of modern man, has given himself. A doctor charts the facts:

> 'Clinical evidence that the heart is irreparably damaged; kidney failure already apparent: Without specific request . . . in my judgement inappropriate to resuscitate.'
>   The nurse beside him read through what he had written.
>   'Nothing else we can do, is there?' The consultant shook his head; 'Pray for a miracle, that's about the only hope. So if he asks for anything, let him have it.'

Another miracle does occur. St Anthony, as it were, is present once more. The 'spirit' to which Morse gave himself throughout his life so fully, coded and silently pointing to another Spirit, is not stocked in the hospital pharmacy, but the Good Samaritan, Morse's long-suffering junior associate, visited: 'someone had already slipped a couple of miniature Glenfiddichs into the top of Morse's bedside table' (RD 347–8). Morse had at one time considered a hymn for his own funeral service. Its title, 'O Love That Wilt Not Let Me Go' (RD 275), might still be fitting, the reader is allowed to hope. At his funeral, it seems, the hymn is sung, there is a promise of the resurrection, and two long-standing enemies at least for a brief time are reconciled (RD 274).

The lost child: How Freud got it wrong

The loss and silence of the Christian tradition in the modern Western world, we have been arguing, is experienced by modernity as the silence of God, but a silence which, if we are attentive, can offer redemptive possibilities. In James' work the break in knowledge of that tradition is paralleled in the treatment of broken familial heritages, and the crises inherited, as it were, by orphaned and adopted children.[107] The breaks that occur in religious traditions, the rejection of a heritage by Daniel Aaron or the discontinuities and resulting losses in the life of Kate Miskin, are repeated in numerous other characters who have lost not only a 'faith tradition' but the parents by whom it could be transferred. To give only a few examples, there is the final tragedy in an attempt to protect an unacknowledged son in *Unsuitable Job for a Woman*. In *Death in Holy Orders*, the suicide at the beginning and Raphael at the close, are both orphans. In *The Murder Room* Neville the psychiatrist who seeks to close the museum – to kill it, one might say – is adopted, and David Wilkins, a minor character who serves an important place in solving the murder is 'trying to connect' (as the characters in E. M. Forster's *Howard's End* are admonished to do) '[w]ith his father and grandfather. With the past. With life' (MR 230), by stealing a painting once in his family's possession and depicting the battle of Passchendaele, where his grandfather died. (On hearing this, Kate, not fully appropriating the lessons she has earlier learned, can only react in *silence*.)

The theme of the adopted child also plays a central role in *A*

Certain Justice and *Original Sin*, as well as other novels, but is most fully developed in James' early work *Innocent Blood*. The novel opens with the central character who, when asked for proof of identity, announces: 'Philippa Rose Palfrey is what I'm called. I'm here to find out who I am' (IB 11). What she discovers is that she is the daughter of child murderers, parents who not only removed their offspring from her past but who closed the future in the destruction of a child. Cut off from the past she can choose only to perfect herself as a model of modern freedom and create herself:

> The advantage of remembering virtually nothing before her eighth birthday, the knowledge that she was illegitimate, meant that there was no phalanx of the living dead, no pious ancestor worship, no conditioned reflexes of thought to inhibit the creativity with which she presented herself to the world. What she aimed to achieve was singularity . . . (IB 12)

Yet she seeks a heritage; she needs, she knows, what her biological mother can give her: 'Information, Knowledge. A past' (IB 41). Without a past, all 'is contrived' (IB 44), 'a whole mythology of identity' (IB 45). Her adoptive father, unable to beget children, is an atheist, separating her from a religious past as well. And yet there is potential for redemption, despite her inherited silence: she can remember a rose garden, her name, and the memory of those Marian images, although neither she nor others in her circle grasp their significance. Her biological father is released on 15 August, the Feast of the Assumption of the Blessed Virgin, a day that leads her, through struggle and sorrow, to find herself, the humble image of her mother with whom she had lived for only five weeks (five decades of this natural rosary), kneeling in a church, to ponder at the least the relationship between love and identity, and with 'unpractised heart' and 'a short untutored prayer' to manifest, perhaps, 'a small accession of grace' to the would-be murderer of her mother (IB 276).

The character of Dalgliesh sums up and extends the problem.

Only an aunt remains to him and she only for a time; his clerical father is long dead. He is a detective, always in search of meaning, a poet, whose work, the novels suggest, is formulated on 'invisible scars' and is directed to 'a case to answer'. 'The very old', he comments, 'make our past. Once they go it seems for a moment that neither we nor they have any real existence' (DD 20). He chooses to be alone, to read by himself and he maintains a 'nostalgic yearning for an England of rural peace . . . a prelapsarian landscape recreated in [Wordsworthian] tranquillity' (MR 23). No one enters his flat on the Thames – life flows by him. He may like being a detective because it allows 'involvement without responsibility' (DD 65; cf. DD 160), working and writing poetry 'to justify self-sufficiency' (BT 12; DHO 266).

Cut off from the past; Dalgliesh has equally lost his future: he is childless, his wife died with his child in childbirth, and in the first novels and the latest ones, his search for answers is linked to the possibility of finding love. What he recognizes is that without a parent, he is in effect not a child. The world of childhood is closed to him: 'But now it suddenly occurred to him that there was a whole territory of human experience on which, once repulsed, he had turned his back, and that this rejection somehow diminished him as a man' (DEW 186). In this simple recognition Dalgliesh is opened to redemption. He is not part of the childless world, as portrayed in James' *The Children of Men* (1992), a world turned to pleasure and technologizing sexual desires so as to forget the end of sexuality. In that novel the last child and only hope of the world is begotten of Luke, the Christian priest (CM 239), the only one with fertile seed who can beget more children and yet the one who gives up his life and its potential for the group. For Dalgliesh there is hope, present even in sentimental closings such as those of James' earliest novels, *Cover Her Face* and *A Mind to Murder*, and in the later ones, *Death in Holy Orders* and *The Murder Room*. In the first even Dalgliesh recognizes the sentimentality of the situation, but, whether '[m]awkish, . . . insincere, . . . [or] an arrogant presumption', he refuses to voice a self-defence and walks 'to the door in silence' (CF 254). And however cloying the end of *The Murder Room* might be for modern matured, enlightened, and less romantic readers, we might do well to consider the mystery of the threefold 'yes' on the final page, the assurance that there is and need be 'No more time', that the lonely departing figures in *Cover Her Face* are together at last (foreshadowed in the togetherness in the last lines of *Original Sin*), and that Emma, the literary critic, and Dalgliesh, the poet, are united and on their way to a mutual 'home'.

Whether overly sentimentalized or not, the love that leads to and makes such a home is a begetting love. Its nature is understood best in the context of the lost child, orphaned and without a future, a theme most fully explored perhaps in the earliest of detective fictions in the West, Sophocles' *Oedipus Tyrannos*. The story unfortunately remains best known in the telling of Sigmund Freud and in the triumph of his therapeutic method by which psychological and individualist concerns are prioritized over political and communal issues. Oedipus (the club-footed and therefore unwanted [?] child) grows to adulthood as an orphan. Not knowing his paternity and hoping to avoid the prophecy that he would kill his father and marry his mother, he leaves home and mistakenly does what he intended not to do. On his journey of escape he meets an older man at a crossroads (for Christians a natural type of the Cross of Christ) who is unwilling to give way, kills him, and turns to Thebes where he marries the widowed queen. When a plague strikes the city, he goes in search of its cause, only to discover the social and political disease infecting the city has its roots in the murder of its King and himself as the killer. He is the detective in search of himself, of an identity lost to him. Freud quite correctly grasped the universality of the narrative's significance, but misses its meaning. An astute literary critic, he too rapidly rushed to read into the tale the story of the emerging twentieth-century sexualized individual and interprets it as the life of every man, seeking to kill his father and marry his mother, arguing the cause of civilization and its discontents in a circular fashion from the libidinous turmoil of the individual and back again.

Freud admits that Oedipus is indeed a 'tragedy of destiny', but he cannot accept what he understands as the traditional reading, namely, that 'its tragic effect is said to lie in the contrast of the supreme will of the gods and the vain attempts of mankind to escape the evil that threatens them. The lesson which, it is said, the deeply moved spectator should learn is submission to the divine will and realization of his own impotence.'[108] The difficulty is that, without the therapeutic procedure of allegorical transference,[109] this does appear to be the reading arising from the text. At the exact centre of the drama, the chorus sums up the issue:

> My lot be still to lead
> The life of innocence and fly
> Irreverence in word or deed,
> To follow still those laws ordained on high
> Whose birthplace is the bright ethereal sky. . . .
> Of overweening pride is bred
> The tyrant; overweening pride full blown . . .
> But the proud sinner, or in word or deed,
> That will not Justice heed,
> Nor reverence the shrine . . .
> grasps at ill-got gain,
> And lays an impious hand on holiest things. . . . [110]

The theme of the play is *hubris*, overweening pride, the desire to be like the gods rather than reverencing them. It is the desire to deny one's origin, to reject the principle that one has an origin, and to pretend that one is oneself, like the gods, one's own origin. It is the refusal to practise the central virtue of the ancient world: *eusebia*, 'reverence', known in the Latin tradition as *pietas*. The chief representative of the ideal Roman, Aeneas, for example, is regularly described in Virgil's *Aeneid*, as *pius Aeneas*, 'pious Aeneas', the one who can lead his son from the burning city of Troy into a future only because he carries his father, Anchises, on his shoulder. Piety is the act of looking back, of recognizing that we are not our own progenitors and that the world we inhabit is a gift offered to us from the past. The just live by grace. It is a humble acknowledgement that if we wish to build a future, we must do so by humbly seeking the advice of those who went, ironically, 'before us' – temporally they preceded us, but spatially they proceed 'before us', opening the path we follow. Oedipus' crime entails his refusal to present a golden bough at the gates of the dead, grasping thereby his own mortality in the mortality of those who gave him birth. The killing of a father, the silencing of tradition, is his denial of a dependence on any other than himself, and his marriage to his mother, his attempt to substantiate that denial by begetting himself, his own arrogant independence of all origins, including those of family and fellow citizens. The desire to be like gods plagues even those cities offered as refuges for the 'original' killers, and because of it *mores* (manners) collapse, and justice with them.

Early in its development Christianity recognized the significance of the supposedly erroneous Septuagint reading of Isaiah 11.2. In the Greek rendering there stood seven gifts of the Spirit as opposed to six according to the letter of Hebrew text. 'Piety' (*eusebia*) was an addition, its source unknown, and whatever the historical reason for its inclusion (the desire of a scribe to have the requisite 'seven' characters, or to justify the copyist's own heritage before his Greek contemporaries), Christians have clung to the alternative reading, even while eliminating it from our now more historically 'accurate' scripture. Without the gift of piety, all other gifts of 'wisdom', 'understanding', 'counsel', and 'knowledge' are self-developed directives to arrogant independent 'might' and a rejection of 'the fear of the Lord' in any form. Without piety, the initial offering of wisdom in particular is lost and perhaps to ensure the maintenance of these two virtues – wisdom and piety – the Christian tradition early linked them in the person of Mary, Dante Alighieri eventually formulating her figure most fully in his *Paradiso* as the redemptive overcoming of Oedipus' crime.

Mary is the 'daughter of her own dear son'. Unlike the pagan

Greek who endeavoured to be his own child, to make his own
future again and again, and thus visits a plague upon his city,
Mary humbly accepts her fulfilment as a human person through
the foreordained grace of her son, and thereby magnifying her
origin and rejoicing in her future, she manifests the universality
of a new city, the citizens of which no longer seek refuge as
would-be gods, but, dying to themselves, humbly love one
another. Daughter of her own dear son, the mother (Mary, the
Church) lives on after the son's murder, since she accepts the role
of daughter (in small part the meaning of that much disputed
dogma of the immaculate conception). There is here at last a
future (eternal life) for the parent since the parent recognizes the
priority of the child, fully freeing the child into its own future,
'letting it be' without origin so that the child might fully
acknowledge the love of its own begetting.

> Vergine Madre, figlia del tuo Figlio,
>   Umile ed alta più che creatura,
>   Termine fisso d'eterno consiglio,
>
> Tu se' colei che l'umana natura
>   Nobilitasti si, che 'l suo Fattore
>   Non disdegnò di farsi sua fattura.
>
>   (Dante, *Paradiso* 33.1–6)

> O Virgin Mother, Daughter of thy Son,
>   Lowliest and loftiest of created nature
>   Fixed goal to which the eternal counsels run,
>
> Thou art the She by whom our human nature
>   Was so ennobled that it might become
>   The Creator to create Himself His creature.[111]

So reads the prayer of St Bernard to the Virgin in the *Paradiso*,
requesting grace for the pilgrim as he strives with wonder 'how to
fit the image to the sphere', his will and desire 'turned by love,

The love that moves the Sun and other stars' – L'Amor che muove il Sole e l'altre stelle (*Paradiso* 33.144–5).

Two absences: Love and death

This long excursus on *Oedipus* and the *Paradiso* may initially appear to have led us far from our theme, but as we have seen in each of the four chapters and in the introduction itself, our task as 'whodunnit' readers has throughout been merged with that of the detective both in search of a fictional murderer, working through the narrative as history to explain the silencing of the victim's voice, and in a parallel exploration, seeking to understand the problem of the silence of God in our time, a problem placed before us in our attempt to follow the Hall directive. As we come to the close of these chapters, we come ever closer as well to the place, like that in the manor-house mysteries of the past, where the evidence is summed up and the parlour-room solution announced.

We begin our summation with the Marian theme and that of love and identity in Dante's *Paradiso*, themes arising almost inevitably at the close of each of our earlier chapters, in each case in minor characters, all waiting and some willing to wait in silence – Emily Wharton and Meg Denison in the first, Janet Carpenter in the second, Daniel Aaron and Kate Miskin in the third. All, with the reader, have been in differing ways in search of the murderer, seeking to understand the particular mystery before them and pressed thereby to consider the wider mystery raised by it in a cultural context in which the primary meanings that once formed that culture and provided explanatory models are dying. The search for the murderer is the search for an explanation of death and the turmoil in which they find themselves. As modern characters they could not, unfortunately, fully theorize their motivations as fixed on the stars, the star of the sea – *maris stella*, Mary, and the love that moves those stars. They live, after all, in a world in which such Christian images are silent and no longer speak to them. The 'Lady Chapels', their proper name and devotional purpose lost, are forgotten at the side of crumbling secular cathedrals. They cannot 'fit the image to the sphere', and yet for some of them, will and desire are 'turned by love'.[112]

Whether it be explicitly 'the love that moves the Sun and other stars' is not made clear for them, but an analogy of such love it appears to be none the less. Love is depicted as the solution against murder, moving outward from the self to the other, toward the public, the community, the whole, the universal, the catholic. As a public act love includes and establishes justice. Thus, in *Unsuitable Job for a Woman* (1972) Cordelia Gray challenges a callous father who is trying to make the world better and thus driving his son to death: 'But what is the use of making the world more beautiful if the people who live in it can't love one another?' (UJW 171). The implication is that purely this-worldly altruistic acts inevitably turn to destroy their own self-created idols, as in *Unnatural Causes* (1967) we are told of 'a useless creature. . . . She was kept and petted by a man who believed that beauty has a right to exist, however stupid, however worthless, because it is beauty. It took only two twitching seconds at the end of a clothesline to dispose of all that nonsense' (UC 240–2).

There is only one way to avoid the outcome: 'Men have either to learn to love each other . . . in the entirely practical and unsentimental use of the word or they will destroy themselves' (UC 121). This Meg Denison in *Devices and Desires* grasps, offering the answer to the murderer, Alice Mair, a woman, who herself lived daily with a twisted manifestation of love, rooted, however passively, in violence and *de facto* murder. Her brother, Alex, knowing she was abused by their father, allowed him to bleed to death after an accident by delaying a call for help, and protected and supported his sister thereafter, setting the stage for further killings. End and means are one, and in spite of the security she has gained through her brother, Alice's life remains, like that of the coroner in *Death of an Expert Witness*, 'anxiety-ridden'. Like him, Alice lives with a corpse always before her, in her case the body of one who was to love, but eliminated love and all proper images of it, leaving his daughter to suffer with a broken model as the only possibility for life. Without love and faced with death daily, the coroner in *Death of an Expert Witness* seeks ways to wash violent reality from his life. He has security, physically and, by allusion, religiously. 'The Old Rectory, inherited from his father, was unmortgaged, unencumbered.' But the theological inheritance is silent, and he is left to cope by his own means:

> [H]e swilled cold water over his hands and arms, then bent down and sluiced the whole of his head. He performed this act of almost ceremonial cleansing before and after every case. He had long ago ceased to ask himself why. It had become as comforting and necessary as a religious ritual, the brief preliminary washing which was like a dedication, the final ablution which was both a necessary chore and an absolution, as if by wiping the smell of his job from his body he could cleanse it from his mind.

He cannot avoid death, of course. He lives without love, or rather, knows it only as an absence: 'Love, the lack of it, the growing need, the sudden terrifying hope of it, was only a burden' (DEW 4–5). As an absence love is a 'want', a lack. Thus, Rose, in *Innocent Blood*, claims she doesn't 'want anything', but in fact does: 'I want to know who I am, I want to be approved of, I want to be successful, I want to be loved' (IB 77). They are things she desires and lacks. And in *A Certain Justice*, Kate's comments: 'Love, always love. Perhaps that's what we're all looking for. And if we don't get it early enough we panic in case we never shall' (CJ 380).

For Alice the problem is similar but greater. She knows love as an absence 'inherited from [her] father' and replaced by the complex (one might say, incestuous) care of her brother. She lives not in a silent Old Rectory, the purpose of which is to house one who seeks the cause of death rather than the celebration of life, but in a Martyr's Cottage, continuously confronted with the appalling death of one who died not for love but, as we have seen, for principle. In the person of Meg Denison she has an opportunity, at the least a model, for redemption.[113] The two sit 'opposite each other' (DD 105). Like the coroner Meg lives and works serving others in an 'Old Rectory', but unlike him the silence of its words is less absolute in that she *serves* there. Her husband died saving the life of another. It is an act of Christian love, even if not explicitly so. She too, in this sense, lives in the inheritance of a martyr, but a martyr of a very different sort. Sadly, it is ineffectual for her grief: '[H]er Christianity was of little help. She didn't reject it, but it had become irrelevant, its comfort only a candle which served fitfully to illumine the dark' (DD 103). And at the close of the novel, when after much agonizing she acts as a mannerly Christian good neighbour in openness even to a murderer, the candle will ignite a destructive blaze for Alice who can understand the act of Meg's husband only in capitalistic terms. Perhaps he 'hadn't died for someone second-rate' (DD 105), she says. What she cannot grasp are actions other than self-interested ones. She cannot understand how, in the face of what she has suffered, Meg can have such an 'extraordinarily benign view of the universe' (DD 106). The comment surprises Meg. She is so un-selfconscious that she is unaware of her prejudices. What she does know, however, is that she has 'always been able to believe that at the heart of the universe there is love'. For Alice, the heart manifests only cruelty, and with Meg's assertion that love is vital for the small child, there is '[a] moment's silence' in which Alice may have glimpsed a saving voice, but turns it to reiterate a self-justifying version of her own life narrative (DD 106).

Seeking the source of love

Sadly, just as death is silent and cannot answer those enquiring after it, so too is love. A commonplace in Western literature from Sophocles to Dante, the linkage of love and death continues in crime fiction as well. In its focus on death the detective story inevitably ponders someone's attempt at a final solution, not grasping its opposite and (in the Christian tradition at least) ultimate overcoming. To take a life is to attempt to be like gods. The fulfilment of a creature, on the opposite hand, is to follow the divine pattern, to die to self in pious recognition of the source of life. The 'final solution' in Christianity is love, proving the ultimate blasphemy of the term's use at Auschwitz and as an argument for Nagasaki.

For characters in James' novels the theme of love as the final solution for death is central. It is the only solution for Cain's original enactment of his parents' sin, but it is often silent and even when enunciated is often confused. A lawyer, in *Innocent Blood*, for example, quotes Thomas Mann: '"For the sake of humanity, for the sake of love, let no man's thoughts be ruled by death." I think I have quoted it correctly, but you get the meaning I'm sure,' and then adds, ignoring the principle: 'That will be fifty pounds' (IB 85). How then does the love to overcome the murderous direction of humanity arise? Not in guilt although this theme is widely treated in James' works.[114] Nor by some individual effort. The psychiatrist in *The Murder Room,* attempting to convince a woman to institutionalize her husband, argues that the husband, if he is capable of understanding, will understand, only to be faced by the response: 'But would he forgive?' The psychiatrist has no answer to the wife's 'Christian' response. He seems to sense that the question of forgiveness is rooted in love, but he cannot separate it from guilt and interprets both as 'emotions', psychological phenomena, not yet fully grasped by his science: 'What was the use, he thought, of trying to persuade her that she should feel no guilt? She was gripped by those two dominant emotions, love and guilt. What power had he, bringing his secular and imperfect wisdom, to purge her of something so deep-seated, so elemental?' (MR 69).[115]

Guilt is a recognition of a state of injustice, perpetuated by human beings in opposition to established human and universal mores. It is not an emotion and no more is love. In the Christian tradition love is the fulfilment of a commandment: 'Behold I give you a new commandment, that you love one another' (John

13.34). For all her limitations, Philippa Rose, the protagonist in *Innocent Blood*, knows this and recognizes that if so, it, like guilt, establishes her psyche but is not determined by it. The commandment to love, she knows, 'wasn't by an act of will'. It is not under the control of the individual. To love is not to comprehend a set of established rules and follow them. In the Christian tradition it is a way. 'Surely the faithful were [then] justified in replying "But Lord, show us how?" And He, the itinerant man/God whom no one would have heard of if he had died sane and in his bed would have had his answer too: "I have".' Love is revealed in death, and there is the model for it. The silence of love, giving itself fully for others, can be understood only in the silence of death. The word is here spoken, and Philippa Rose hears it in spite of her setting. It comes to her while reflecting on the 'humourless' chaplain at her 'nominally a Christian' school in which 'Anglicanism, particularly High Anglicanism, was accepted as a satisfying compromise between reason and myth, justified by the beauty of its liturgy, a celebration of Englishness, . . . essentially . . . the universal religion of liberal humanism laced with ritual to suit each individual taste', and the few others, 'Roman Catholics, Christian Scientists and Nonconformists were regarded as eccentrics governed by family tradition.' The café in which the words came to her 'was not the most suitable place for the resolution of a moral dilemma. The noise', the reader is told, 'was appalling' (IB 93–4); silencing one might suppose any divine voice, she takes up the task of detective and goes in search of her origins.

In the search that Philippa Rose undertakes, she discovers she is the child of a murderer, a child murderer, no less. She is at once the orphan-victim (cut off from her parents and her heritage of meaning in the Rose garden, the earliest memory she has) and the detective-interpreter. But there is more and this, Philippa Rose grasps as well. In the four preceding chapters we have stood as readers and detective-interpreters outside the narratives, following with, alongside and sometimes leaping ahead of the detective. The reader, the detective, the critic-interpreter are pursuing one and the same activity, seeking to discover the mystery lurking behind the deaths depicted and the mystery of their meaning, and in so doing, like Philippa Rose, to write a narrative, either substantiated or rejected on the basis of the evidence offered at the close of the novel, and thereby left to write the greater narrative of the fuller mystery into which the search for the murderer and the phenomenon of Cain leads.

Two decades ago, in his postscript to *The Name of the Rose*, Umberto Eco reflected on a then recent critical judgement that 'of all possible murder-story situations . . . there is still to be written a book in which the murderer is the reader'.[116] Then, offering his reader brief pause to begin a new paragraph, Eco concluded: 'Moral: there exist obsessive ideas, they are never personal: books talk among themselves, and any true detection should prove that we are the guilty party.'[117]

We need not explore in detail Eco's postmodernist contentions here on the nature of the person and the literary construction of truth. In the first place he moves too quickly in associating the individual reader in the first statement to the detective-critics in the moral, the 'we' whose individual liability is limited by the guilty group within which they sit at ease. Within that group an individual reader can enjoy life as a detective, seeking rhetorical indulgence for his crimes, loving nothing better than to 'curl up with a good book'. The book in this case is secondary to the event – it is, as we already noted, consumable. By so doing one can avoid social responsibilities and enter a world of one's own, even using a search for the author's intention to serve only as an opportunity for escape. Reading is the most private of acts – quite unlike theatre or concert attendance that require the presence of others and performers alike, unlike viewing and listening to recorded films and music that directly challenge one's eye or ear and unlike poetry that demands oral and aural externals to live. Second, Eco makes no mention that the murder story in which the murderer is the reader *has been written*. It is the Christian narrative, the biblical collection in which the books of Sacred Scripture and Tradition consistently 'talk among themselves' about the greatest murder of all time: the killing and silencing of God. As a universal narrative, the Christian story includes all human narratives, and because of the central question it raises and the nature of that question it allows all those particular narratives their own freedom. The question is not 'Who did Jesus die for?' with the aberrant self-indulgent answer 'me', an objective case to whom things are done and who can then rest assured that the greater authority rules. The question is rather 'Who killed Jesus, the Word?' with humbled reflection: 'I', the reader, the case under which all else in the sentence is subjected. I killed the word, by defining it, by controlling it, by not being attentive and open to the words' leading, by silencing its voice with my own and asserting my own interpretative act against that of the Word's body, the catholic, universal whole in the image of the one who humbly heard and bore the universe within her womb. Whether or not there are 'good' books is difficult to say. That there can be good readers is another matter – in the latter case, one and the same person declares justice and, co-operating with the declaration, is freed from binding fictions.

It is common for readers of fiction to identify with the characters, and in the reading of detective fiction, the commonest practice is to follow in the path of the detective, adjudicating oneself as successful against or alongside the superior model of the sleuth. The practice, however, is self-serving. If one chooses the detective as model, one chooses the authoritative position. As James describes Dalgliesh, he is 'a very detached man, essentially a very lonely man in a lonely profession, one which brings him into contact with tragedy, with evil'. He is then, not surprisingly, an artist, the one who understands his role as standing outside a situation and viewing it objectively: 'At the same time, he has the sensitivity of a poet, which I think makes him a complex character and the reconciliation of these two very different facets of his character is interesting.'

I think the interaction of human beings in a closed society is absolutely fascinating: the power struggles, the attempt to establish and retain one's own identity, the way in which people group in defensive or offensive alliances, particularly against strangers. And I think, too, that there's a certain dramatic element in the detective coming into this society, penetrating it, seeing it with fresh eyes – and the whole society reacting to him.[118]

As a result, Dalgliesh must face the frightening risk of 'rejection', above all the willingness 'to *accept* the momentous presumption that Emma loved him' (MR 26; emphasis mine). 'Love is dangerous. . . . You're only half alive if you're afraid to love' (MR 351), we are told.

It is the task of the detective to discover what has happened, to sort out the evidence, arrive at a conclusion and pass on the knowledge to judicial process. To have knowledge is to stand above a situation and to remain in control of it. Even in *A Certain Justice*, in which he cannot bring the perpetrator to justice, Dalgliesh knows who is guilty. To be a detective is to be the one at the centre, the reader-interpreter, the judge of those fragments of the religious tradition remaining in one's world. But this, in effect, is the act of Cain: the desire to speak. It is Oedipal, not Marian love. Dalgliesh's struggle at the close is to overcome his professional orientation and live in silence, acknowledging that he cannot stand outside the social construct as his own creation, but that he is part of it. And as part of it, he, like the victim in the larger body of detective fiction, is the murderer. Such an acknowledgement is confession, and only in full confession, in full recognition of one's communion with humanity as a whole, lies the possibility of redemption. On the universal plane confession so fully accepts individual participation in the fallenness of humanity at its origin that its word is a silent 'let it be', and, open to a new creation, the acceptance of the 'momentous presumption' that one is loved. In that single act of confession one remembers one's origin in Cain and is released in silence to hear with thanks the Word of one's remembered and loving Creator. With acceptance of the sin as personal, there is no sin; it exists only then as forgotten in the way in which ignorance passes with the coming of knowledge. We have an analogy in *Death of an Expert Witness* with a murderer's confession:

> It wasn't love, but it was in its own way a kind of loving. And it was such peace. This is peace, too, knowing that there's nothing else I need do. There's an end of responsibility, and end of worry. A murderer sets himself aside from the whole of humanity for ever. It's a kind of death. I'm like a dying man now. The problems are still there, but I'm moving away from them into a new dimension. (DEW 264–5)

Something of that new dimension may be seen in the allusions in the final scene in *Death in Holy Orders* with which we opened this chapter – the allusion to the apostolic succession in Raphael, the orphaned child of a murderer, ordained a good priest by the traditional laying on of hands, and in the white smoke, an indication that a new universal pastor has been chosen to protect the deposit of traditional faith as a servant of servants of Christ, a servant of the Church, in the humble, silent, and loving pattern of the totality of that body, Mary. The voice of the past is silent. The great institution is at an end.[119] What will become of the Anglo-Catholic tradition and the many gifts it bore and might have borne to the Church as a whole is unknown to either of the remaining witnesses. Their remembrance will no longer be perpetuated in human words; that word is silent. Generation proceeds not from word to ear (such an act occurred only once), but in the community established from hand to shoulder. With his ordination Raphael will voice a new angelic song, not as his own but in the person of another (*in persona Christi*), by, in, and through whom alone he will enact in remembrance (*anemnesis*) a sacrifice of praise, giving thanks (*eucharistesas*) and promising peace (*pax vobiscum*), making present again the body of the Victim who does not victimize and in whom all parts speak not with their own destructive voices but in unity and communion with one Word, the light-giving creative *Fiat* of his divine Father

(*Fiat lux*) in the humble, wise, and loving, human *Fiat* of his Mother, 'Thy will be done' – *Fiat voluntas tua*. Hereafter all that can be brought to memory, piously re-'membered' into an unknown future, is a liturgical cult (*cultus*, worship) by which thanksgiving is daily offered for the final mystery of divine release (*missa est*, it is sent, and only in such a way is it ended), expressed as the silent love and service of a Lord above and beneath a fallen culture and on which the hope of a new culture may as silently arise.[120]

And so we close. With an act of thanksgiving, not speech. With remembrance in silence of a silenced, murdered Word, risen and to come again. In hope beyond proof.[121] Can Christian faith be harmonized with contemporary thought, as John Albert Hall asked? Can the Christian Word crucified continue to seek to bring faith where there is no faith, give strength to faith where faith is weak, and offer joy to faith where faith is strong, when all its sound during this long Holy Saturday of Western Christianity seems to be driven out to the edges of reality? It is said that in religion the metaphor establishes belief, in literature it 'cannot claim to do more than to "suspend" our disbelief'.[122] Perhaps it is so. But perhaps not. Perhaps even in our literary escapes into silence a larger hand reaches forward to our smaller shoulders. In James' novel, *The Black Tower*, there is an echo heard in Dalgliesh's mind, the voice of an elderly, now silenced, murdered priest, Father Baddely: 'This is the spiritual life; the ordinary things one does from hour to hour' (BT 22). Among the ordinary things, one might include the reading of crime fiction, and perhaps in the moments it offers us to suspend our disbelief, analogically, at the closure of each novel, we may confess our limitations with warm remembrance and thanksgiving for acceptance – at the very least, acceptance by a writer who allowed us for a silent hour or two to ponder unexpected mysteries.

Notes

1. Note Dennis Porter, *The Pursuit of Crime: Art and Ideology in Detective Fiction* (New Haven: Yale University Press, 1981), 7, on the 'consumption' of detective fiction (working from Stanley Fish, *Self-Consuming Artifacts: The Experience of Seventeenth Century Literature* (Berkeley, Calif.: University of California Press, 1972)). Detective fiction at large is widely discussed and outlined. For some recent important general works (in addition to those in notes below), see Lee Horsley, *Twentieth-Century Crime Fiction* (Oxford: Oxford University Press, 2005), Stephen Thomas Knight, *Crime Fiction, 1800–2000: Detection, Death, Diversity* (New York: Macmillan, 2004), John Scaggs, *Crime Fiction* (London: Routledge, 2005), Carl Darryl Malmgren, *Anatomy of Murder: Mystery, Detective, and Crime Fiction* (Bowling Green, Ohio: Bowling Green State University Popular Press, 2001), Rosemary Herbert, *The Fatal Art of Entertainment: Interviews with Mystery Writers* (Toronto: Maxwell Macmillan Canada, 1994). With particular respect to this study see Heta Pyrhönen, *Mayhem and Murder: Narrative and Moral Problems in the Detective Story* (Toronto: University of Toronto Press, 1999). On women writers and issues see Christine A. Jackson, *Myth and Ritual in Women's Detective Fiction* (Jefferson, N.C.: McFarland & Co., 2002), Gill Plain, *Twentieth-Century Crime Fiction: Gender, Sexuality and the Body* (Chicago: Fitzroy Dearborn, 2001), Maureen T. Reddy, *Sisters in Crime: Feminism and the Crime Novel* (New York: Continuum, 1988), Kathleen Gregory Klein, *The Woman Detective: Gender and Genre* (2nd edn, Urbana: University of Illinois Press, 1995), Kimberly J. Dilley, *Busybodies, Meddlers, and Snoops: The Female Hero in Contemporary Women's Mysteries* (Westport, Conn.: Greenwood Press, 1998), Mary Hadley, *British Women Mystery Writers: Authors of Detective Fiction with Female Sleuths* (Jefferson, N.C.: McFarland & Co., 2002).

Notes

2. See W. H. Auden, 'The Guilty Vicarage' (1948), in Robin W. Winks (ed.), *Detective Fiction: A Collection of Critical Essays* (Woodstock, Vt.; Countryman Press, 1988), 15–24.

3. The pattern was well established. It was as old as the Gothic romance (see especially Matthew Lewis, *The Monk* (1796)) and reached its heights, one might argue, in that most formidable Canadian literary success, *Awful disclosures of Maria Monk, as exhibited in a narrative of her sufferings during a residence of five years as a novice and two years as a black nun, in the Hotel Dieu Nunnery at Montreal* (London: Richard Groombridge, 1836, among many other editions of the same year; the volume has been regularly in print since its initial publication and remains widely circulated in both print and electronic copies).

4. Of these there are no end of examples: for a few see John Case, *The Genesis Code* (1997), Alan Folsom, *Day of Confession* (1998), Paul Adam, *Unholy Trinity* (1999), Lewis Purdue, *Daughter of God* (2001), Philip Kerr, *Dark Matters* (2002), Bartholomew Gill, *Death in Dublin* (2003), Dan Brown, *The Da Vinci Code* (2003) and his earlier *Angels and Demons* (2000), David Hewson, *A Season for the Dead* (2003), Robert Goddard, *Days without Numbers* (2003), Daniel Silva, *The Confessor* (2003), Richard Montanari, *The Rosary Girls* (2005), Steve Berry, *The Third Secret* (2005), Kate Mosse, *Labyrinth* (2005), and on. Note also Papal interest generally in this regard: Peter De Rosa, *Pope Patrick* (1995), Andrew Greeley, *White Smoke: A Novel about the Next Papal Conclave* (1996), and the far better work by Morris West, *The Shoes of the Fisherman* (1964) and *Eminence* (1998). Compare the much earlier comic piece by Robert Ludlum, *The Road to Gandalfo* (1992). For an example of a similar rhetoric, depending on implicit fears and long-standing prejudices but applied to other Christian communities in the 'serious' novel, see Margaret Atwood's *The Handmaid's Tale* as both novel (1986) and opera (2003), a work unexplainable aside from popular misconceptions regarding 'Fundamentalist', 'Bible-belt', and 'Moral Majority' Christianity.

5. For some examples of works with few religious implications beyond their titles note: Stephen Dobyns, *Church of Dead Girls* (1997), John Harvey, *Last Rites* (1998), Elizabeth Corley, *Requiem Mass* (1998), Denise Mina, *Sanctum* (2002), Tess Gerritsen, *The Sinner* (2003).

6. John Shelby Spong, *Why Christianity Must Change or Die: A Bishop Speaks to Believers in Exile* (San Francisco: Harper, 1998). Compare, on the Canadian scene, the rapid rise and fall of Tom Harper's *The Pagan Christ: Recovering the Lost Light* (Toronto: Thomas Allen, 2004).

7. For the proposal see Francis Lacassin, *Mythologie du Roman Policier* (2 vols.; Paris: Union Générale d'Editions, 1974) and the remarks

on the relationship between the crime novel and modern industrial society in his edited collection, *Entretiens sur la paralittérature* (Paris: Plon, 1970), 1:18.

8. For a full listing of texts cited and materials on James referenced see the bibliography below. *The Lighthouse* appeared after the Hall Lectures were delivered. For other works on James see the interviews with Patricia Craig, 'An interview with P. D. James, detective fiction', *Times Literary Supplement*, 5 June 1981, 641–2, and Dale Salwak, 'An Interview with P. D. James', *Clues: A Journal of Detection 6/1* (1985), 31–50; Richard B. Gidez, *P.D. James* (Boston: Twayne, 1986), and Bruce Harkness, 'P. D. James', in *Art in Crime Writing: Essays in Detective Fiction*, ed. Bernard Benstock (New York: St Martin's Press, 1983), 119–41.

9. John Albert Hall was a parishioner at St Paul's Anglican Church (formerly the naval and garrison church, later moved to its present location), Esquimault, British Columbia, in which a plaque remains to his memory: 'To the Glory of God and in the Memory of Lieut[enant]-Col[onel] John Albert Hall 1868–1932.' I am thankful to Douglas Henderson of Esquimault, who kindly introduced me to the church.

10. Note in this respect the comments of Porter: 'The example of her work reminds us, in fact, how in one form or another mass popular literature invariably takes upon itself the ideological function of transmitting a *doxa*. Moreover, in a post-religious society like that of modern Britain, it is frequently the only kind of widely-read material that attempts to distinguish between right or wrong or set up models to be imitated. And among all forms of popular literature, nowhere is this more true than in detective fiction in the broad sense. Where else outside detective fiction does it still seem appropriate to raise questions about such theological categories as "good" and "evil" or such philosophical ones as "truth" and "justice"?' (Dennis Porter, 'Detection and ethics: the case of P. D. James', in Barbara A. Rader and Howard G. Zettler (eds), *The Sleuth and the Scholar: Origins, Evolution, and Current Trends in Detective Fiction*, Contributions to the Study of Popular Culture, 19 (New York: Greenwood Press, 1988), 11–18 at p. 12.) Note the peculiar treatment of James by Norma Siebenheller (*P. D. James* (New York: Frederick Ungar, 1981)), who makes no mention of the religious element in her study, and the similar pattern in the argument of Michael O'Hear and Richard Ramsey ('The detective as teacher: didacticism in detective fiction', *Clues: A Journal of Detection* 21 (2000), 95–104), who point to the use of some detective fiction (Hillerman, McBain, Gash, and Kemelman) to pass on accurate information about something along with their tales of murder.

11. As raised in *The Verbal Icon: Studies in the Meaning of Poetry* by

Notes

W. K. Wimsatt, Jr, and Monroe C. Beardsley (Lexington: University of Kentucky Press, 1954).

12. 'Theological aesthetics' is most succinctly defined by Gesa E. Thiessen as 'concerned with questions about God and issues in theology in the light of and perceived through sense knowledge, . . . through beauty and the arts' in the introduction to her edited *Theological Aesthetics* (London: SCM Press, 2004), 1. For a fascinating 'long elliptical essay in theological aesthetics' see David Bentley Hart, *The Beauty of the Infinite: The Aesthetics of Christian Truth* (Grand Rapids, Mich.: William B. Eerdmans, 2003); Hart offers a perhaps better definition of theological aesthetics than does Thiessen in the question that he states 'prompted' his work: 'Is the beauty to whose persuasive power the Christian rhetoric of evangelism inevitably appeals, and upon which it depends, theologically defensible?' (1). In this context note as well John Milbank, Graham Ward, and Edith Wyschogrod, *Theological Perspectives on God and Beauty* (Harrisburg, Pa.: Trinity, 2003). For a useful survey of more recent theoretical approaches see Luke Ferreter, *Towards a Christian Literary Theory* (London: Palgrave, 2003) and for a fine example of a contemporary study, briefly treated by Ferreter, see Paul S. Fiddes, *Freedom and Limit: A Dialogue between Literature and Christian Doctrine* (Macon, Ga.: Mercer University Press, 1999). A more general approach is that of Paul Avis, *God and the Creative Imagination: Metaphor, Symbol and Myth in Religion and Theology* (London: Routledge, 1999). The differences regarding 'mystery' between my own reflections and Fiddes' may be in part explained by his use of Tillich and Rahner (31). In large part my interests are shaped by those of Hans Urs von Balthasar, initially summed up in his *The Glory of the Lord, vol. I: A Theological Aesthetics*, trans. Erasmo Leiva-Merikakis (Edinburgh: T&T Clark, and San Francisco: Ignatius Press, 1982), 441ff. On the complexities of an incarnational reading of a literary work see the early work of William F. Lynch, *Christ and Apollo: The Dimensions of the Literary Imagination* (New York: Sheed & Ward, 1960) and the detailed discussions and bibliography in Francesca Aran Murphy, *Christ the Form of Beauty: A Study in Theology and Literature* (Edinburgh: T&T Clark, 1995). Useful considerations of theology and literature by novelists are available in John Gardner, *On Moral Fiction* (New York: Basic Books, 1978), Annie Dillard, *Living by Fiction* (New York: Harper, 1982), Andre Dubus, *Broken Vessels* (Boston: David R. Godine, 1991), and Ron Hansen, *A Stay against Confusion: Essays on Faith and Fiction* (New York: HarperCollins, 2001). Compare as well in a differing mode the stimulating thoughts of Robert Calasso, *Literature and the Gods*, trans. Tim Parks (London: Vintage, 2001).

Notes

13. John Buchan, *The Thirty-Nine Steps* (Edinburgh: Blackwood, 1915), v.

14. See above all Simone Weil, 'Reflections on the right use of schools studies with a view to the love of God', in *Waiting on God*, trans. Emma Crawford (London: Routledge & Kegan Paul, 1951).

15. Note her comment: 'Perhaps the chief reason why I am glad to have these three early books reissued in hardcover is that each was a landmark in my own gradual realization that, despite the constraints of this fascinating genre, a mystery writer can hope to call herself a serious novelist' (*Crime Times Three* (New York: Charles Scribner's Sons, 1979), viii). For a good treatment of James as a serious novelist see Ulrich Suerbaum, 'Neues vom Krimi? P. D. James und die Veredelung des Detektivromans', *Anglistik und Englischunterricht* 37 (1989), 7–31, the reflections in Maurizio Ascari, 'Fantasmi jamesiani nel post-moderno', *Poetiche: Letteratura e Altro* 2 (1996), 57–68, Richard I. Smyer, 'P. D. James: crime and the human condition', *Clues: A Journal of Detection* 3/1 (1982), 49–61, and cf. Rosemary Herbert, 'A mind to write', *Armchair Detective: A Quarterly Journal Devoted to the Appreciation of Mystery* 19/1 (1986), 340–8, at 341, and John Leonard, 'Conservative fiction(s): P. D. James' *The Black Tower' Journal of Australasian Universities Language and Literature* 83 (1995), 31–41, at 31. On James and religion see the short reflections in Samuel Coale, *The Mystery of Mysteries: Structural Differences and Designs* (Bowling Green, Ohio: Bowling Green State University Popular Press, 2000), 13–21, and his 'Carnage and conversion: the art of P. D. James', *Clues: A Journal of Detection* 20/1 (1999), 1–14.

16. The words are those of Charles Gore, Principal of Pusey House, Oxford, and the editor of the volume, *Lux Mundi: A Series of Studies in the Religion of the Incarnation* (Cambridge: Cambridge University Press, 1889), preface, 1–2. For overviews of the project see Peter Hinchliff, *God and History: Aspects of British Theology 1875–1914* (Oxford: Clarendon, 1992), 99–121, the classic study by Arthur Michael Ramsey, *From Gore to Temple: The Development of Anglican Theology between Lux Mundi and the Second World War 1889–1939* (London: Longmans, 1960), and Robert Morgan (ed.), *The Religion of the Incarnation: Anglican Essays in Commemoration of Lux Mundi* (Bristol: Bristol Classical Press, 1989).

17. Note the argument of Penelope K. Majeske, 'P. D. James' dark interiors', *Clues: A Journal of Detection* 15 (1994), 130, regarding *A Taste of Death*: 'If the text does not conclude that faith cannot be sustained in the twentieth century, it almost certainly is a story about the decline of the old social order which once affirmed it. In Kate Miskin and Darren

Notes

Wilkes, it celebrates the new order, however spiritually frail they may be.'

18. The definition is that of the British Prime Minister, William E. Gladstone (1809–98), in his *The State in its Relations with the Church* (London: John Murray, 1838), 1:11.

19. For details see Ramsay Cook, *The Regenerators: Social Criticism in Late Victorian English Canada* (Toronto: University of Toronto Press, 1985), 49.

20. For useful reflections on the political implications of our post-Constantinian age for Christians see Stanley Hauerwas, *With the Grain of the Universe: The Church's Witness and Natural Theology Being the Gifford Lectures delivered at the University of St. Andrews in 2001* (Grand Rapids, Mich.: Brazos Press, 2001) and the critique by Jeffrey Stout, *Democracy and Tradition* (Princeton, N.J.: Princeton University Press, 2004).

21. Shakespeare, *Romeo and Juliet*, Act 2, scene 2. Among the many volumes treating the changes that mark modernity see above all Charles Taylor, *Sources of the Self: The Making of the Modern Identity* (Cambridge: Cambridge University Press, 1989), as well as Louis Dupré, *Passage to Modernity: An Essay in the Hermeneutics of Nature and Culture* (New Haven: Yale University Press, 1993) and *The Enlightenment and the Intellectual Foundations of Modern Culture* (New Haven: Yale University Press, 2004), William C. Plancher, *The Domestication of Transcendence: How Modern Thinking about God went Wrong* (Louisville, Ky.: Westminster John Knox Press, 1996), and note the debates over secularized Christian forms in Karl Löwith, *Meaning in History* (Chicago: University of Chicago Press, 1949) and Carl Schmitt, *Political Theology: Four Chapters on the Concept of Sovereignty*, trans. George Schwab (Cambridge, Mass.: MIT, 1985), with the counter-arguments of Hans Blumenberg, *The Legitimacy of the Modern World*, trans. Robert M. Wallace (Cambridge, Mass.: MIT, 1982) and Marcel Gauchet, *The Disenchantment of the World: A Political History of Religion*, trans. Oscar Burge (Princeton: Princeton University Press, 1997).

22. For a full discussion of the relationships between Christianity and atheism note, above all, Michael J. Buckley, *At the Origins of Modern Atheism* (New Haven: Yale University Press, 1987) and his *Denying and Disclosing God: The Ambiguous Progress of Modern Atheism* (New Haven: Yale University Press, 2004), noting as well the critique by John Milbank in *Modern Theology* 8 (1992), 89–92.

23. For further details see Stanley Jaki, *Lord Gifford and His Lectures: A Centenary Retrospective* (Mercer, Ga.: Mercer University Press, 1986).

Notes

24. For a superb description of this phenomenon see Max Picard, *The Flight from God*, trans. Marianne Kuschnitzky and J. M. Cameron with introductions by Gabriel Marcel and J. M. Cameron (Washington: Regnery Gateway, 1951; first published in German, 1941).

25. On the initial use of the term as denoting 'a-religious' see G. J. Holyoake, *The Principles of Secularism Briefly Explained* (London: Holyoake & Co., 1859).

26. I have deliberately chosen to characterize the problem with Nagasaki rather than Hiroshima, because in the latter instance, I recognize (although I do not accept the argument) that a case might be argued for the aggression.

27. It is to this phenomenon that *Silence*, the remarkable novel (trans. William Johnson (Tokyo, 1969)) set in Nagasaki by the Japanese Christian, Shusaku Endo, directs our attention. For fuller recent and differing treatments on the theme see the essays in *Silence and the Word: Negative Theology and Incarnation*, ed. Oliver Davies and Denys Turner (Cambridge: Cambridge University Press, 2002) and note as well Rachel Muers, 'Silence and the Patience of God', *Modern Theology* 17 (2001), 85–98.

28. For abbreviations see Bibliography below.

29. Thereby the strikingly puritanical emphases of secularist options in which the rhetoric of justification (as a process including sanctification) is replaced by a static 'justice' language according to which rights can be judicially chartered and judged. Consistent with this approach is its tendency to deterministic or fatalist (predestinarian?) interpretations of criminality, for example, as the result of social or psychological factors (except in the case of the secularist's enemies) and the dependence on models of therapeutic refashioning of human behaviour rather than on transformative ideals. It is as if Luther's 'simul iustus et peccator' adage is read forensically with respect to the first term, but morally with respect to the second.

30. For the distinction between purpose and meaning, I am dependent here on the argument of Romano Guardini, *The Spirit of the Liturgy*, trans. Ada Lane (New York: Benzinger, 1931), 90: 'The conception of purpose regards an object's center of gravity as existing outside that object, seeing it lie instead in the transition to further movement, i.e., that towards the goal which the object provides. But every object is to a certain extent, and many are entirely, self-sufficient and an end in itself – if, that is, the conception can be applied at all in this extensive sense. The conception of meaning is more adaptable. Objects which have no purpose in the strict sense of the term have a meaning. This meaning is not realized by

their extraneous effect or by the contribution which they make to the stability or the modification of another object, but their significance consists in being what they are. Measured by the strict sense of the word, they are purposeless, but still full of meaning. Purpose and meaning are the two aspects of the fact that an existent principle possesses the motive for, and the right to, its own essence and existence. An object regarded from the point of view of purpose is seen to dovetail into an order of things which comprehends both it and more beyond it; from the standpoint of meaning, it is seen to be based upon itself.'

31. For other reviews of the problem see Charles Taylor, *The Malaise of Modernity* (Toronto: Anansi, 1991).

32. Note the place of the ecological theme in this respect in DD 43, 49, 64, and passim.

33. See Porter, 'Detection and ethics', 17 for details.

34. G. K. Chesterton, 'The Quick One', in *The Scandal of Father Brown* (Harmondsworth: Penguin, 1978; 1st edn, 1929), 24.

35. On James' preference for the term 'crime novel' see Patricia A. Ward, 'Moral ambiguities and the crime novels of P. D. James', *Christian Century* 101 (16 May 1984), 519–22. In this respect compare the wide range of critics who note the religious and moral elements in James' work. For a brief overview of the history see Julian Symons, *Bloody Murder: From the Detective Story to the Crime Novel: A History* (London: Faber & Faber, 1972; Harmondsworth: Penguin, 1974) and the classic articles on the mystery in Robin W. Winks, *Detective Fiction: A Collection of Critical Essays* (Woodstock, Vt.; Countryman Press, 1988); Edmund Wilson, 'Who cares who killed Roger Acroyd?' (1950), 35–40; Joseph Wood Krutch, 'Only a detective story' (1944), 41–6; Dorothy Sayers, 'The omnibus of crime' (1929), 53–83.

36. Note the other reflections in James' work on this theme. In UJW 191, after Cordelia helps the killer of the murderer make the act appear to be a suicide, the murderess says: 'Death is the least important thing about us. Comfort yourself with Joseph Hall: "Death borders upon our birth and our cradle stands in the grave".' See also the play on the theme in the fourth book of DHO and DEW 32: 'Death isn't terrible. Murder is. Death isn't; at least, no more than birth is.'

37. The title to Dalgliesh's first volume of poetry, *Invisible Scars,* is significant in this respect. The detective, like Eliot's 'wounded surgeon' (see Leonard, 'Conservative fiction(s)?', 12) must cut to cure the disease. On some of the many allusions to Eliot in James see Betty Richardson, '"Sweet Thames, Run Softly": P. D. James's *Waste Land* in *A Taste for Death*', *Clues: A Journal of Detection* 9 (1988), 105–18. The wide use of

literary references in James' work supports this call for retrieval. See Delphine Kresge Cingal, 'Intertextuality in the detective fiction of P. D. James: literary game or strategic choice?' *Clues: A Journal of Detection* 22/2 (2001), 141–52 and S. L. Clark, '*Gaudy Night's* legacy: P. D. James' *An Unsuitable Job for a Woman*', *The Sayers Review* 4/1 (1980), 1–12.

38. George Grant, *Lament for a Nation: The Defeat of Canadian Nationalism* (Toronto: McClelland & Stewart, 1970; 1st edn, 1965), 97. Cf. the conclusion to Grant's *Time as History*, Massey Lectures, Ninth Series (Toronto: Canadian Broadcasting Corporation, 1969), 52, and the similar yet very different, hopeful, and 'liberal' project of 'retrieval' by Charles Taylor in his *Sources of the Self*: 'The intention of this work was one of retrieval, an attempt to uncover buried goods through rearticulation – and thereby to make these sources again empower, to bring the air back again into the half-collapsed lungs of the spirit' (520). Cf. as well the conclusion to Taylor's *Hegel and Modern Society* (Cambridge: Cambridge University Press, 1979).

39. Cf. Eric Nelson, 'P. D. James and the dissociation of sensibility', in *British Women Writing Fiction*, ed. Abby H. P. Werlock (Tuscaloosa: University of Alabama Press, 2000), 56–69, Nicola Nixon, 'Gray areas: P. D. James's unsuiting of Cordelia', in Glenwood Irons (ed.), *Feminism in Women's Detective Fiction* (Toronto: University of Toronto Press, 1995), 29–45, Sue Ellen Campbell, 'The detective heroine and the death of her hero: Dorothy Sayers to P. D. James', in Irons, *Feminism*, 29–45, 12–28 (see also *Modern Fiction Studies* 29 (1983), 497–510), and Kathleen Gregory Klein, 'Truth, authority, and detective fiction: the case of Agatha Christie's *The Body in the Library*', in Jerilyn Fisher and Ellen S. Silber, *Analyzing the Different Voice: Feminist Psychological Theory and Literary Texts* (Lanham, Md.: Rowman & Littlefield, 1998), 103–16.

Note as well the discussion regarding the place of Cordelia Gray in James' novels. Joan G. Kotker, 'The re-imagining of Cordelia Gray' in Klein, *Women Times Three*, argues that Dalgliesh grows in the novels, but Gray does not and that the Gray of UJW is realistic but in *The Skull Beneath the Skin* she is 'flat, simplistic, and unconvincing'. Kotker then goes on to chide James for her treatment of Gray and suggests that James is doing this because she is against extreme feminists. Note that in the Jane S. Bakerman interview ('"From the time I could read, I always wanted to be a writer": Interview with P. D. James', *Armchair-Detective: A Quarterly Journal Devoted to the Appreciation of Mystery, Detective, and Suspense Fiction* 10 (1977), 55–7, 92; and cf. Jane S. Bakerman, 'Cordelia Gray: apprentice and archetype', *Clues: A Journal of Detection* 5 (1984), 101–14), James defines herself as a feminist because she likes

Notes

women, but not as an extreme one. (Cf. Kotker, 'Re-imagining', 63 and note also Joan G. Kotker, 'P. D. James's Adam Dalgliesh Series', in Mary Jean DeMarr (ed.), *In the Beginning: First Novels in Mystery Series* (Bowling Green, Ohio: Bowling Green State University Popular Press, 1995), 139–53, outlining James' move away from the traditional detective story.) Campbell however sees her as developing Gray in *The Skull Beneath the Skin* and moving away from the Sayers' novel formula which James also uses. Nixon sees Gray in UJW as a 1970s feminist foil for Dalgliesh (Nixon, 'Gray Areas', 30) and reads the Gray in *The Skull Beneath the Skin* as a proto-Thatcherite and anti-feminist figure for the new era (Nixon, 'Gray Areas', 44).

For James' own comment on the matter see Susan Rowland's précis of her remarks: 'I invited Lady James to give her opinion of feminism. She replied by emphasising that she liked and respected her own sex. Firmly believing in equality based upon economic liberation and the control of fertility, she did refer to a "shadow side" to reforms. For example, easier divorce has entailed inflicting suffering upon children. In disliking "the extremes of feminism", she said that radical feminism had done harm to relations between women and men. When I suggested that *A Certain Justice* seemed preoccupied with the problems of mothering for professional women, Lady James agreed that that was a concern in the novel, but made a crucial distinction between didacticism and literature. She was not, she said, a feminist writer in the sense of driving through a didactic project to show the problems of women in the modern world. Nevertheless, she believed that modern young women were under great strain in the effort to combine motherhood with career expectations' (Susan Rowland, *From Agatha Christie to Ruth Rendell: British Women Writers in Detective and Crime Fiction* (Basingstoke: Palgrave, 2001), 197).

40. The problem has been notably raised by Roman Catholic writers. For useful insights see above all the comments by the novelists David Jones, 'Art and sacrament: an enquiry concerning the arts of man the Christian commitment to sacrament in relation to contemporary technocracy', in Lady Pakenham (ed.), *Catholic Approaches* (London: Weidenfeld and Nicolson, 1955), 143–84, Georges Bernanos, 'Christianity and the writer's task: letter to Frédéric Lefèvre', *Communio* 28 (Spring 2001), 202–10, and Elizabeth Jennings, *Christianity and Poetry* (London: Burns & Oates, 1965) as well as the commentaries collected in J. C. Whitehouse (ed.), *Catholics on Literature* (Dublin: Four Courts, 1997). Note as well the secondary reflections by Nicholas Boyle, *Sacred and Secular Scriptures: A Catholic Approach to Literature* (Notre Dame: University of Notre Dame Press, 2004).

Notes

41. As quoted in the Martin Wroe interview in *Book & Culture* (March/April 1998), 14–15.

42. James, 'The art of the detective novel', 7. Note as well her interview comment: 'I can write quite quickly. It is the plotting and planning which take the time and those can't be hurried. It's as if the characters exist already, their story, everything about them is in some limbo of my imagination and I'm getting in touch with them and getting the story down in black and white, rather than inventing any of it. So it does feel as if it's a process of revelation rather than creation and one which is not really within my own volition' (Antje Mosebach, '"A smell of the place should almost rise from the pages": P. D. James and London – An Interview', *Anglistik und Englishunterricht* 54 (1994), 178).

43. Joseph Conrad, *Nigger of the Narcissus*, 'Introduction'. My boldness in 'reading out' from an author within the Christian tradition owes much to the practice of Hans Urs von Balthasar in his *Bernanos: An Ecclesial Existence*, trans. Eramso Leiva-Merikakis (San Francisco: Ignatius Press, 1996) and *Tragedy under Grace: Reinhold Schneider on the Experience of the West,* trans. Brian McNeil, CRV (San Francisco: Ignatius Press, 1997), as well as those studies in *The Glory of the Lord*, vol. III: *Studies in Theological Style: Lay Styles*, trans. Andrew Louth, John Saward, Martin Simon, and Rowan Williams (Edinburgh: T&T Clark; San Francisco: Ignatius Press, 1986) and elsewhere.

44. In this I argue in a very different way from those authors who suppose that the relationship between theology and detective fiction is that they both come to 'conclusions' about 'meaning', 'human nature', etc., nor am I following the thematic approach of Robert D. Paul, 'Theology and detective fiction', *Student World* 55 (1962), 186–95 and 'Theology and detective fiction', *Hartford Quarterly* 6 (1966), 21–9. For a general review of religious mysteries see William David Spencer, 'Religious mysteries', in Robin W. Winks and Maureen Corrigan (eds), *Mystery and Suspense Writers: The Literature of Crime, Detection, and Espionage* (2 vols; New York: Charles Scribner's Sons, 1998), 2:1161–81 and note as well Charlotte Whittingham, 'Christian ritual and creed in Åke Edwardson's *Gå ut min själ*', *Crime Scenes: Detective Narratives in European Culture since 1945*, ed. Anne Mullen and Emer O'Brien (Amsterdam: Radopi, 2000), 113–24.

45. On the place of liturgy in this respect see Catherine Pickstock, *After Writing: On the Liturgical Consummation of Philosophy* (Oxford: Blackwell, 1998).

46. For details see Taylor, *Sources of the Self*.

47. For a readable and highly insightful treatment of this patristic

Notes

method of interpretation and its relation to mystery as I have outlined it here, see Andrew Louth, *Discerning the Mystery: An Essay on the Nature of Theology* (Oxford: Clarendon, 1983; rpt in paperback, 1999). This path to theological truth, followed with an eye ever drawn to the beauty of God, never failed in the history of Christian life and, although sometimes disregarded by more aggressive travellers, has in recent times regained attention. Pre-eminent among its supporters is the Swiss Catholic theologian Hans Urs von Balthasar (1905–88) and a variety of followers and compeers in Catholic, Orthodox, Anglican, and Protestant communities.

48. For the fullest study of the fourfold approach to interpretation see Henri de Lubac, *Histoire et Esprit: L'intelligence de l'Écriture d'après Origène* (Paris: Aubier, 1950), *Exégèse médiéval: Les quatre sens de l'Écriture* (4 vols; Paris: Aubier, 1959–64), now in the process of translation into English. Note as well the selections in Henri de Lubac, *Scripture in the Tradition*, trans. Luke O'Neill (New York: Herder & Herder, 1968) and the study by Susan K. Wood, *Spiritual Exegesis and the Church in the Theology of Henri de Lubac* (Grand Rapids, Mich.; Eerdmans, 1998). For a wider discussion of the question see Stephen E. Fowl (ed.), *The Theological Interpretation of Scripture: Classic and Contemporary Readings* (Oxford: Blackwell, 1997) and Rowan Williams, 'The discipline of Scripture', in *On Christian Theology* (Oxford: Blackwell, 2000), 44–59.

49. For further discussion see Ernst Robert Curtius, 'Brevity as an ideal of style', in *European Literature and the Latin Middle Ages*, trans. Willard R. Trask (New York: Harper & Row, 1953), 487–94.

50. Augustine, *Confessions*, trans. William Watts (London and Cambridge, Mass.: William Heinemann and Harvard University Press, 1951), 12:24.

51. Cf. the essays by Annie Dillard, *Living by Fiction* (New York: Harper & Row, 1982). Note James' character, Conrad Ackroyd, a Roman Catholic, who comments to Dalgliesh that he 'should read detective fiction. Real-life murder today, apart from being commonplace, and – forgive me – a little vulgar, is inhibiting of the imagination' (MR 7). Likewise, her DHO is worked out around the diary of a woman who has lost her faith but is trying to overcome the horror of seeing a death (suicide) by 'writing it down as if it were fiction' – at the advice of a local priest (DHO 3).

52. For another approach to 'reading' in the sense developed here see Paul J. Griffiths, *Religious Reading: The Place of Reading in the Practice of Religion* (New York: Oxford University Press, 1999).

53. It is in this sense I think that Chesterton's comments were meant: 'The criminal is the creative artist; the detective only the critic' ('Blue cross', 12). 'A crime . . . is like any other work of art. . . . [C]rimes are by no means the only works of art that come from the infernal workshop. But every work of art, divine or diabolic, has one indispensable mark – I mean that the centre of it is simple, however much the fulfillment may be complicated' ('The queer feet', in *The Innocence of Father Brown*, 72).

54. Note the words of Wilfrid Sheed in this respect: 'It's the odd case against symbols: if you get them they seem obvious and artificial, and if you don't, you miss the whole point' (*The Good Word and Other Words* (Harmondsworth: Penguin, 1980, 130). Note the struggle of James' character Kate Miskin, who has lost Christian faith and thus finds Dalgliesh's poetry a mystery (MR 221), and the comment that the detective is accordingly a sort of priest 'without the confidentiality of the confessional and no absolution' (DD 314).

55. Chesterton, 'Blue Cross', 17.

56. London: Macmillan, 1996. For a succinct biography, review of Dexter's work, and parallels between the author and his chief character see Douglas G. Greene, 'Colin Dexter (b. 1930)', in Winks and Corrigan, *Mystery and Suspense Writers*, 1:291–99.

57. For their place in the Anglo-Catholic liturgy see *Ritual Notes: A comprehensive guide to the rites and ceremonies of the Book of Common Prayer of the English Church, interpreted in accordance with the latest revisions of the Western use* (10th edn; London: W. Knott, 1956, among numerous editions from 1897).

58. Note as well the same title for Book Four in TD.

59. In this respect note the introduction to *The Murder Room* and the quotation from T. S. Eliot: 'Time present and time past/ Are both perhaps present in time future/ And time future contained in time past.' On the ever-present martyr to science in *Devices and Desires*, see also DD 107, 151.

60. Cf. DD 66–7, 124, 230.

61. See, for example, John G. Cawelti, *Adventure, Mystery, and Romance: Formula Stories as Art and Popular Culture* (Chicago: University of Chicago Press, 1976), 104, who argues that the detective story offers readers 'temporary release from doubt and guilt, generated at least in part by the decline of traditional moral and spiritual authorities, and a rise of new social and intellectual movements that emphasised the hypocrisy and guilt of respectable middle-class society'.

62. P. D. James 'The art of the detective novel', *New Welsh Review* 5 (1989), 9. Note as well her concluding remarks in the interview by White

with the detective novelist Laurence Block. When asked about the attraction to the mystery genre she replied:

'Because they do affirm the intelligibility of the universe; the moral norm; the sanctity of life. And because, at the end, there is a solution. I think I'm very frightened of violence. I hate it. I'm very worried by the fact that the world is a much more violent place than when I was a girl. And it may be that by writing mysteries that I am able, as it were, to exorcize this fear, which may very well be the reason why so many people enjoy reading a mystery. It seems to me that the more we live in a society in which we feel our problems – problems of war and peace, racial problems, problems of drugs, problems of violence – to be literally beyond our ability to solve, it seems to me very reassuring to read a popular form of fiction which itself has a problem at the heart of it. One which the reader knows will be solved by the end of the book; and not by supernatural means or good luck, but by human intelligence, human courage and human perseverance. That seems to me one of the reasons why the crime novel, in all its forms and varieties, does hold its place in the affections of its readers . . .' (Terry White, 'No gore, please – they're British', New York Times, 9 October 1988, Section 7: 1).

63. Note as well her comment in Diana Cooper-Clark, *Designs of Darkness: Interviews with Detective Novelists* (Bowling Green, Ohio: Bowling Green State University Press, 1983), 18: the interviewer suggests that crime fiction is 'to release the reader from the anxieties of the modern world. . . . [to] ease the modern reader's sense of impotence' and James rejects the notion: 'No I don't. I am surprised I said that actually because I don't think that is what I am trying to do.'

64. Compare Baudelaire's verse in which this aestheticized transcendence collapses in the 'decayed' Christian tradition out of which it lives.

> Car c'est vraiment, Seigneur, le meilleur témoignage
> Que nous puissons donner de notre dignité
> Que cet ardent sanglot qui roule d'âge en âge
> Et vient mourir au bord de votre éternité!

> (For clearly, Lord, the clearest proofs
> That we can give of our nobility,
> Are these impassioned sobs that through the ages roll,
> And die away upon the shores of your Eternity.)

Notes

Charles Baudelaire, 'Les Phares (The Beacons)', in *The Flowers of Evil*, French edition by Yves-Gérard Le Dantex, trans. William Aggelier (Fresno, Calif.: Academy Library Guild, 1954), 30–1.

65. My play on the biblical title and the Chalcedonian formula is deliberate, shaped somewhat by my reading of Richard Bauckham, *God Crucified: Monotheism and Christology in the New Testament* (Grand Rapids, Mich.: Eerdmans, 1998).

66. 'What James seeks is that essential man, a common humanity, however ambiguous and self-serving, in all its complexities and complicities. . . . It is this pursuit which fuels her dark fictions. The manners and the essential human matter exist in an uncertain equilibrium in regard to one another, but from the carnage of her vision, she pursues the conversion of her characters, readers and probably herself, as she initiates the rites of mystery over and over again, playing out the ritual of exorcism and possible redemption, despite the fact that she recognizes that blood is never innocent, that original sin contaminates our devices and desires, and that we all have a taste for death' (Coale, 'Carnage and conversion', 12).

67. On the permanent removal of a victim's body as the final act of a murderer see the forthcoming book *A Doctor's Calling: A Matter of Conscience*, by John Gradon and Hazel J. Magnussen on the murder of Ms Magnussen's brother. I am thankful to Ms Magnussen for informing me of the book and providing me with a draft of the typescript.

68. The lower-case 'c' is deliberate. I include within the definition all Christian ecclesial communities owning the central creedal traditions of the fourth and fifth centuries.

69. Umberto Eco, 'The poetics of the open work', in *The Role of the Reader: Explorations in the Semiotics of Texts* (Bloomington, Ind.: Indiana University Press, 1984; 1st edn, 1979), 65. Compare other essays in this work, particularly 'Narrative structures in [Ian] Fleming', 144–72, and related pieces in his *The Open Work*, trans. Anna Cancogni (Cambridge, Mass.: Harvard University Press, 1989), 22–3. Among Eco's essays of direct interest to my argument see *The Aesthetics of Chaosmos: The Middle Ages of James Joyce,* trans. Ellen Esrock (Cambridge, Mass.: Harvard University Press, 1989; 1st Italian edn, 1962), *Travels in Hyperreality*, trans. William Weaver (San Diego, Calif.: Harcourt, Brace, Jovanovich, 1986), *Art and Beauty in the Middle Ages*, trans. Hugh Bredin (New Haven: Yale University Press, 1986; 1st Italian edn, 1959), and *The Aesthetics of Thomas Aquinas*, trans. Hugh Bredin (Cambridge, Mass.: Harvard University Press, 1988; 1st Italian edn, 1970).

70. Trans. William Weaver (San Diego, Calif.: Harcourt, Brace, Jovanovich, 1983). As to the implications for Christianity see Eco's

Notes

Postscript to the Name of the Rose (San Diego, Calif.: Harcourt, Brace, Jovanovich, 1984; included in the 1994 paperback edition), 503–36 and [Cardinal] Carlo Maria Martini and Umberto Eco, *Belief or Nonbelief? A Confrontation* (New York: Arcade, 2000).

71. On Eckhart's thought see Bernard McGinn, *The Mystical Thought of Meister Eckhart: The Man from Whom God Hid Nothing* (New York: Crossroad, 2001).

72. Flannery O'Connor, *Collected Works*, ed. Sally Fitzgerald (New York: Library of America, 1988), 934. Cf. the theme of James' 'Manners and murder: women detective writers as social historians', presented at the Margaret Howard Memorial Lecture, 15 May 2003, St Cross Building, Oxford.

73. See Hanna Charney, *The Detective Novel of Manners: Hedonism, Morality, and the Life of Reason* (Rutherford: Fairleigh Dickinson University Press, 1981), xi, and note also George Grella, 'Murder and manners: the formal detective novel', *Novel* 4 (1970), 30–48.

74. See James' comments in Cooper-Clark, *Designs of Darkness*, 19.

75. P. D. James in the Bakerman interview, 56.

76. Much of James' early work, for example, plays in varying ways with the form, satirizing and reformulating it before redirecting the formulae her 'summary' reprints in the collection, *Murder in Triplicate*. The volume appeared as an American imprint under the title *Crime Times Three: Three Complete Novels featuring Adam Dalgliesh of Scotland Yard: Cover Her Face, A Mind to Murder, Shroud for a Nightingale* (New York: Charles Scribner's Sons, 1979). Note the way in which a country house has been turned into a laboratory in James' *Death of an Expert Witness* (1977; cf. Bernard Benstock, 'The clinical world of P. D. James', in Thomas F. Staley (ed.), *Twentieth-Century Women Novelists* (Totowa, NJ: Barnes & Noble, 1982), 104–29) and a Wren chapel has been deconsecrated – 'ideals of order, beauty, and faith of former times' turn out to be places of murder as Porter, 'Detection and ethics', 17, notes.

77. Cf. Charney: As in the novel of manners 'in detective novels the normal order is revealed to have been, to a certain extent, an appearance' (*The Detective Novel of Manners*, 91).

78. London: Collins, 1959; 1st edn 1957. For quotations see 39–40.

79. Ibid., 256.

80. The allusion here to Martha C. Nussbaum, *The Fragility of Goodness: Luck and Ethics in Greek Tragedy and Philosophy* (Cambridge: Cambridge University Press, 1986) is deliberate. Note in particular the critical review by Charles Taylor in the *Canadian Journal of Philosophy* 18 (1988), 805–14.

81. A favourite saying of James, as Herbert notes, 'A mind to write', 341.

82. For details see Paul Althaus, *The Theology of Martin Luther* (Philadelphia, Pa.: Fortress Press, 1966).

83. James Lee Burke, *Black Cherry Blues* (New York: Avon, 1989), 242–3. On the collective mediating structure of the community and the Church see *Sunset Limited* (New York: Island Books, 1998), 164, and compare the reflections in his *A White Stained Radiance* (1992; New York: Avon, 1993), 336–8.

84. Even less likely would Luther's more liberal descendants be pleased with the intercessory prayers of Burke's hero (*Black Cherry Blues*, 195) and the pattern of his confessions (ibid., 187; *Heaven's Prisoners* (New York: Pocket Books, 1989), 114f.; *Heartwood* (New York: Island, 1999); *White Doves at Morning* (1st edn, 2002; New York: Pocket Star, 2004), 427–9), among other religious reflections in his novels.

85. Compare James Lee Burke, *Last Car to the Elysian Fields* (New York: Pocket Books, 2003), 430: 'Clete had made a point, one which I don't think was either vituperative or vain. Legal definitions had little to do with morality. It was legal to systemically poison the earth and sell arms to Third World lunatics. Politicians who themselves had avoided active service and never had listened to the sounds a flame thrower extracted from its victims, or zipped up body bags on the faces of their best friends, clamored for war and stood proudly in front of the flag while they sent others off to fight it. The polluters and the war advocates are always legal men, as the Prince of Darkness is always a gentleman.'

86. Cooper-Clark, *Designs of Darkness*, 23.

87. Mosebach, 'A smell of the place', 179–80. Note also James' response in the interview to a question regarding the significance of architecture in her work: 'All the places where [the characters] live fulfil the function of the plot and of characterization, and they have a symbolic importance, too' (179). It is in this context, perhaps, that one might best interpret her comment near the conclusion of the interview that the interior is the person (183). On this matter see also Patricia A. Ward, 'Moral ambiguities and the crime novels of P D James', *Christian Century* 101 (16 May 1984), 519–22. It is the importance of this communal aspect and its relation to the individual that Leonard confuses in his treatment: 'James . . . grounds her fiction on the gloomy basis of the flawed nature of humanity. In this world of *Original Sin*, murder is not even, perhaps, an individual, free choice, but simply an index of the radical sinfullness of the world' (32). 'But . . . [James] is not prepared to bring into question the view that the root of crime is to be located in the individual, flawed soul,

instead of in the socialized and social life of the individual: her "reason and order" are neither so reasonable nor ordered as she would have us believe' (39). They are certainly not 'so reasonable and so ordered'; her works do not require this conclusion. Note the similar difficulty of Erlene Hubly, 'The formula challenged: the novels of P. D. James', *Modern Fiction Studies* 29 (1983), 515: 'James opens [her early novel] up to all the complexities of the social scene, a move that has certain consequences for the novels to follow. For it makes it increasingly difficult for her to sustain the two assumptions upon which the classical detective novel is based: (1) that the world is a limited place in which all things can be known and explained; and (2) that the world is a good and orderly place.' The same inability to escape Enlightenment prejudices is evident in the reflections of Susan Rowland, 'The horror of modernity and the utopian sublime: Gothic villainy in P. D. James and Ruth Rendell', in Stacy Gilles and Philippa Gates (eds), *The Devil Himself: Villany in Detective Fiction and Film* (Westport Conn.: Greenwood, 2002), 133: 'P. D. James and Ruth Rendell are both detective writers in the tradition of the literary Gothic. Although they both deploy Gothic terrors to represent villainy as socially implicated, they produce radically differing visions of culture and crime. James' reactionary Gothic embodies a horror of secular modernity: societies that abandon the manifesting of moral order through traditional Christianity cannot secure justice. By contrast, Rendell's liberal politics creates crime plots that become increasingly aware of political injustices surrounding the structuring of cultural differences of class, gender and ethnicity. The dawning of a radical social vision within the fiction occurs in ways that suggest more enlightened social possibilities that cannot yet be directly represented in the crime and detecting genres. For Rendell, the Gothic sublime enables the representation of desire as problematic, as excessive to social and familial conventions, and, crucially, as excessive to the resources of literary conventions to exhaust its significance. Gothic villains thereby serve to critique cultural norms such as those of class and gender. Her Gothic villainy shows that desire demands something more, it demands social transformation.' Rowland here properly describes the thrust of James' novels, but mistakenly supposes that modernity can separate itself from its Christian heritage. Note the similar confusion on Rowland's part in her interview with James and Rowland's seeming inability to grasp the implications of James' comments regarding faith and certainty: 'At the mention of the morality play, I put it to Lady James that this particular traditional form is necessarily metaphysical: it presupposes a sacred dimension of reality to underpin its moral absolutes. This dimen-sion is not represented in her work, despite her personal membership of the Anglican Communion and her interest in portraying believers in her novels. Was this part of her devotion to realism in her art (and not to the more self-referential aspects of the golden age genre)? Does it correspond to her personal religious attitude? Lady James admitted that this modification to the implications of a morality play was indeed part of her commitment to literary realism. She described her religious attitude as not one of "certainty": no one can be 100 per cent certain of metaphysical truths. There are huge areas pertaining to faith that cannot be securely "known". Religious certainty can be dangerous and can lead to fanaticism, which she is concerned to avoid' (Susan Rowland, *From Agatha Christie to Ruth Rendell: British Women Writers in Detective and Crime Fiction* (Basingstoke: Palgrave, 2001), 197).

88. P. D. James, 'Dorothy L. Sayers: her novels today', *Seven: An Anglo American Literary Review* 10 (1993), 29.

89. Milagros Sanchez-Arnosi, 'El crimen o la fascinacion por el enigma', *Cuadernos Hispanoamericanos: Revista Mensual de Cultura Hispanica* 464 (1989), 125–8.

90. Note the conversation between Piers and Kate in *A Certain Justice*:

'What does this theology do for you? After all, you spent three years on it. Teach you how to live? Answer some of the questions?'
'What questions?'
'The big questions. The ones there's no sense in asking. Why are we here? What happens when we die? Have we really free will? Does God exist?'
'No, it doesn't answer questions. It's like philosophy, it tells you what questions to ask.'
'I know what questions to ask. It's the answers I'm after. And what about learning how to live? Isn't that philosophy too? What's yours?'
The reply had come easily but, she had thought, with honesty: 'To get as much happiness as I can. Not to harm others. Not to whine. In that order.' (CJ 305)

Note as well CJ 210 and DHO 199, where Piers admits to himself that he didn't tell the whole truth to Kate why he studied theology at Oxford – that it was simpler to get in than was history –

He didn't tell her either what it was he chiefly gained: a fascination with the complexity of the intellectual bastions which men could construct to withstand the tides of disbelief. His own disbelief had remained unshaken, but he had never regretted those years.

91. For fuller contemporary discussion of the theme see above all Jean-Luc Marion, *God without Being*, trans. Thomas A. Carlson (Chicago: University of Chicago Press, 1991) and *The Idol and Distance*, trans. Thomas A. Carlson (New York: Fordham, 2001).

92. Note the comment of Sizemore, 'The city as mosaic', 187, suggesting that the mosaics reflect 'the value of human connection, given only perhaps by grace as their association with churches implies'. Note as well Pamela Marks, 'Mine eyes open: anti-romance in P. D. James's *Innocent Blood*', *Clues: A Journal of Detection* 21/1 (2000), 73–86.

93. Compare the way in which the eye is forced from left to right in the description of the portrait in James' *The Black Tower* (1975), 45–6. Dalgliesh here is entering hell and with his guide (interestingly enough bearing the surname 'Court', representing the manners of the court) is not offered the possibility of looking up or down, except in the one case where such an image, the staircase, is immediately overshadowed by humanity's own attempt at rising by its own mechanism, the elevator. Even the hope of angels turns the eye to human concerns. Nor do the Pre-Raphaelite depictions (noted elsewhere, as well, by James; cf. DHO 55, 141) provide the inhabitants with interpretative possibilities, aside from their immediate message: expulsion and death.

In DHO 61 (cf. DHO 54, 165), the painting of 'the Doom' is described first iconically from above to below and then from right to left, the scales demanding justice on St Michael's left, whereas the righteous are on the viewer's left; the first thing the viewer sees is salvation, St Michael's sword of the spirit, enacting righteousness. 'The Virgin and Child', the Holy Family altarpiece, on the other hand, is what will endure. The lamp of the eternal presence burns before it (the eye moves down and up as in the case of an icon (DHO 63)) before and after the discovery of murder, even though St Anselm's (a particularly loved form of the church) is 'doomed' – note the parallel columns between which both 'Doom' and the seminary are seen (Doom, 169; the seminary, 203). On the impact of screen capitalism on religion, one may consider the 'reading' of 'Doom' on the part of the Archdeacon, who sees in it only cash value and that of Father Sebastian (DHO 77, 125).

94. James' work reflects this problem of flat-screen reality at a number of points besides those discussed below. Note her concern over film versions of her work in TE 200–1 and her concern with portrayals of violence (TE 139 and 103). She cannot suspend her disbelief faced with the film's intensification of reality; and the way in which that medium twists reality became clear to her in her first 'real-life' meeting with Tony Blair (236; cf. Dalgliesh's first meeting with the elder Treeves in DHO 14).

Notes

On the topic generally, compare as well the comments of Burke's Robicheaux, who reflects after returning from Mass: 'Television programs treat the legal process as an intelligent and orderly series of events that eventually punishes the guilty and exonerates the innocent. The reality is otherwise. The day you get involved with the law is the day you lose all control over your life. What is dismissed by the uninitiated as "a night in jail" means sitting for an indeterminable amount of time in a holding cell; with a drain hole in the floor, looking at hand-soiled walls scrawled with pictures of genitalia, listening to other inmates yell incoherently down the corridors while cops yell back and clang their batons on the bars' (James Lee Burke, *Purple Cain Road* (New York: Dell, 2000), 282).

Note as well James' comment that in the film version of *A Certain Justice* 'more I fear will be lost than parts of the plot' (TE 68, and 158–9; Piers Tarrant, the 'theologian', is dropped), and the extensive use of the theme of psychopathic voyeurism in the book; in the early 'scenes' of the work the accused and the lawyer work together like excellent actors, picking up cues, in this travesty of justice.

95. Cf. Oliver O'Donovan's *Common Objects of Love: Moral Reflection and the Shaping of Community* (Grand Rapids, Mich.: Eerdmans, 2002), 45ff.

96. One might note the technique in John Updike's *In the Beauty of the Lilies* (New York: Knopf, 1996), in which the author imitates the various styles of the novel through the twentieth century as his plot develops over that period, the latter sections 'reading' much more quickly than the former.

97. My reflections on the text here owe much for their inspiration although not their content to *Van den Gheesteliken Tabernakel*, among other works by the thirteenth-century mystic, Jan van Ruusbroec. See *Werken*, ed. J. B. Poukens, L. Reypens *et al.* (4 vols.; Tielt: Lannoo, 1944–8). For a short readable introduction on his life and work see Paul Verdeyen, *Ruusbroec and his Mysticism*, trans. André Lefevre (Collegeville, Minn.: Liturgical Press, 1994).

98. 'For me, psychopathic murderers are the most frightening' (P. D. James, Review: *The Reason Why: An Anthology of the Murderous Mind*, edited by Ruth Rendell, *Sunday Times Books*, 8 October 1995, Section 7).

99. The term is Gillian Rose's. See her full study, *The Broken Middle: Out of Our Ancient Society* (Oxford: Blackwell, 1992) and her use of the term in *Mourning Becomes the Law: Philosophy and Representation* (Cambridge: Cambridge University Press, 1996). Note as well her autobiographical reflections, *Love's Work* (London: Chatto & Windus, 1995).

Notes

100. "'Ideas of the Cavern are the Ideas of every Man in particular; we every one of us have our peculiar Den, which refracts and corrupts the Light of Nature, because of the differences of Impressions as they happen in a Mind prejudiced or prepossessed." Francis Bacon, Novum Organum Scientarum, Section II, Aphorism V' (IF 197).

101. 'The Character of Compliance: "The Idols of the Theatre have got into the human Mind from the different Tenets of Philosophers and the perverted Laws of Demonstration. All Philosophies hitherto have been so many Stage Plays, having shewn nothing but fictitious and theatrical Worlds." Francis Bacon, Novum Organum Scientarum, Section II, Aphorism VII' (IF 373).

102. My argument here regarding the fictional character Anthony Wood's historiography does not neglect his own self-appraisals as an historian and related passages at IF 534, 561, 596, 619, 631, all of which can be read as the expected apologetic among those who uphold the view here described.

103. Note the use of the word 'truth' in the New Catholic Catechism, in which almost all references to the term are in the exposition of this commandment.

104. John Henry Newman, *The Idea of a University*, 7:10.

105. Colin Dexter, *The Remorseful Day* (London: Macmillan, 1999).

106. Note as well the angelic possibilities in RD 345: 'Were angels male or female? They'd started off life as male, surely? So there must have been a sort of trans-sexual interim when ... Morse's mind was *wondering* [emphasis mine; not 'wandering'] ... What gender was the Angel of Death then, whom he now saw standing at the right-hand side of his bed, with a nurse holding one gently restraining hand on a softly feathered wing, and the other hand on his own shoulder.'

107. Cf. the theme in the title of James' 'On being the prodigal son', in *Our Childhood's Pattern: Memories of Growing up Christian*, ed. Monica Furlong (London: Mowbray, 1995).

108. Sigmund Freud, *The Interpretation of Dreams*, trans. James Strachey (New York: Avon, 1965), 295.

109. That is the use of metaphor by which one topic is 'carried across' into a dissimilar one, rather than a typological interpretation (such as that of the traditional fourfold method) by which one attends analogically to the manifold meanings in the literal text (*sensus plenior*).

110. Translation adapted from Sophocles, *Oedipus the King*, trans. Francis Storr (Loeb Library Edition; Cambridge, Mass., and London: Harvard University Press and William Heinemann, 1912).

111. Dante Alighieri, *The Comedy: Cantica III: Paradise*, trans.

Notes

Dorothy L. Sayers and Barbara Reynolds (Harmondsworth: Penguin, 1962); translations hereafter from the same work.

112. 'Many of my books are – well, they're to do with death – but they're also to do with love, different aspects of human love' (as quoted in Herbert, 'A mind to write', 348). On the issue see as well the comments by Porter: 'The only salvation for all those teeming, lost souls that P.D. James's intrigues of crime and violence uncover in contemporary society is a religion of love, of devotion and sacrifice of self, the love of a parent for a child. But this is precisely what is lacking in the world projected in her fiction' (Porter, 'Detection and ethics', 16). She 'clings to one central concept of Christian faith, namely Pauline *charitas*. That is why her sense of "personhood" is very different from E. M. Forster's liberal humanist affirmation of "personal relations"' (Porter, 'Detection and ethics', 17).

113. She will have it again at the close of the narrative when Meg takes the evidence to her, as we have seen, in the earlier chapters.

114. See the Bakermann interview, 'From the time I could read', 55–6 and cf. her 1986 statement: 'My new novel is about guilt. I think guilt is a fascinating subject altogether, because to be human is to be guilty, whether the guilt is rational or not. I think perhaps the difference between the cozy detective story and the modern detective story – which may also be called the crime novel – is that the latter does turn its attention to this question of guilt' (Herbert, 'A mind to write', 344).

115. Compare as well his psychologizing of guilt in 'some words I'd read written by a philosopher, I think Roger Scruton. "The consolation of imaginary things is not imaginary consolation." I told him I sometimes craved even imaginary consolation. Neville said we have to learn to absolve ourselves. The past can't be altered and we have to face it with honesty and without excuses, then put it aside; to be obsessed by guilt is a destructive indulgence. He said that to be human is to feel guilt: "I am guilty therefore I am"' (MR 238–9).

116. OuLiPo, 'Ouvroir de Littérature Potentielle' (Workshop for Potential Literature).

117. Umberto Eco, 'Postscript', in *The Name of the Rose*, trans. William Weaver (San Diego: Harcourt Brace, 1994), 535.

118. Bakerman, 'From the time I could read', 56. James' comments on the observatory status of the writer needs careful consideration in this light. Note her comments in ibid., 55: 'I think writers always stand outside and observe. . . . one stands outside one's own experience even. One is able, even at moments of tragedy, to be watching it – to be suffering even. I think this is essential to a writer. One is in society, as we all are, but at the same time detached and watching.'

Notes

119. On the need to face certain 'unpalatable facts' about the Church, see as early a word as CF 27. On the importance of institutions and structures in James' work see Sandra Pla, 'P. D. James: a new queen of crime', *Caliban* 23 (1986), 81. Note the place of the underground and the maze of streets in London and elsewhere in her work (cf. Christine Wick Sizemore, 'The city as mosaic: P. D. James', in her *A Female Vision of the City: London in the Novels of Five British Women* (Knoxville: University of Tennessee Press, 1989), 152–87 and of place in James, 'The art of the detective', 6) — a mark of underground psychology? or an underground as past and hiddenness of life generally?

120. On the union of the liturgical and the mystical, the divine and the human Christ in Jan van Ruusbroec's theology of the way from humanity to divinity, see Paul Mommaers, *The Riddle of Christian Mystical Experience: The Role of the Humanity of Jesus* (Louvain: Peeters, 2003) and compare Mark A. McIntosh, *Mystical Theology: The Integrity of Spirituality and Theology* (Oxford: Blackwell, 1998).

121. Note, in this respect, the novel by Laurence Cosse, *A Corner of the Veil*, trans. Linda Asher (New York: Scribner, 1999), in which a proof for God's existence is discovered and society is shattered.

122. John Coulson, *Religion and Imagination: 'In Aid of a Grammar of Assent'* (Oxford: Clarendon Press, 1981), 32.

Bibliography

Alighieri, Dante. *The Comedy: Paradise*, trans. Dorothy L. Sayers and Barbara Reynolds. Harmondsworth: Penguin, 1962.

Ascari, Maurizio. 'Fantasmi jamesiani nel post-moderno', *Poetiche: Letteratura e Altro* 2 (1996): 57–68.

Augustine. *Confessions*, trans. William Watts. London and Cambridge, Mass.: William Heinemann and Harvard University Press, 1951.

Avis, Paul. *God and the Creative Imagination: Metaphor, Symbol and Myth in Religion and Theology*. London: Routledge, 1999.

Bakerman, Jane S. 'Cordelia Gray: apprentice and archetype', *Clues: A Journal of Detection* 5/1 (Spring–Summer 1984): 101–14.

Bakerman, Jane S. '"From the time I could read, I always wanted to be a writer": interview with P. D. James', *Armchair-Detective: A Quarterly Journal Devoted to the Appreciation of Mystery, Detective, and Suspense Fiction* 10 (1977): 55–7, 92.

Benstock, Bernard. 'The clinical world of P. D. James', in *Twentieth-Century Women Novelists*, ed. Thomas F. Staley, 104–29. Totowa, NJ: Barnes & Noble, 1982.

Bernanos, Georges. 'Christianity and the writer's task: letter to Frédéric Lefèvre', *Communio* 28 (Spring 2001): 202–10; trans. David Christopher Schindler from Bernanos, *Essais et écrits de combat*, vol. I (Paris: Editions Gallimard, 1971), 1048–55.

Blake, Nicholas. *End of Chapter*. London: Collins, 1959 [1957].

Burke, James Lee. *Last Car to the Elysian Fields*. New York: Pocket Books, 2003.

Burke, James Lee. *Purple Cain Road*. New York: Dell, 2000.

Burke, James Lee. *Black Cherry Blues*. New York: Avon, 1989.

Calasso, Robert. *Literature and the Gods*, trans. Tim Parks. London: Vintage, 2001.

Bibliography

Campbell, Sue Ellen. 'The detective heroine and the death of her hero: Dorothy Sayers to P. D. James', in *Feminism in Women's Detective Fiction*, ed. Glenwood Irons, 12–28. Toronto: University of Toronto Press, 1995. See also *Modern Fiction Studies* 29 (1983): 497–510.

Charney, Hanna. *The Detective Novel of Manners: Hedonism, Morality, and the Life of Reason*. Rutherford: Fairleigh Dickinson University Press, 1981.

Chesterton, G. K. 'Blue cross', in *The Scandal of Father Brown*. Harmondsworth: Penguin, 1978 [1929].

Chesterton, G. K. 'The queer feet', in *The Scandal of Father Brown*. Harmondsworth: Penguin, 1978 [1929].

Chesterton, G. K. 'The quick one', in *The Scandal of Father Brown*. Harmondsworth: Penguin, 1978 [1929].

Clark, S. L. '*Gaudy Night's* legacy: P. D. James' *An Unsuitable Job for a Woman*', *The Sayers Review* 4/1 (1980): 1–12.

Coale, Samuel. *The Mystery of Mysteries: Structural Differences and Designs*. Bowling Green, Ohio: Bowling Green State University Popular Press, 2000.

Coale, Samuel. 'Carnage and conversion: the art of P. D. James', *Clues: A Journal of Detection* 20/1 (1999): 1–14.

Conrad, Joseph. *The Nigger of the 'Narcissus': A Tale of the Forecastle*. London: William Heinemann, 1897.

Cooper-Clark, Diana. *Designs of Darkness: Interviews with Detective Novelists*. Bowling Green, Ohio: Bowling Green State University Press, 1983.

Coulson, John. *Religion and Imagination: 'In Aid of a Grammar of Assent'*. Oxford: Clarendon Press, 1981.

Craig, Patricia. 'An interview with P. D. James. Detective fiction', *Times Literary Supplement* (5 June 1981): 641–2.

Davies, Oliver, and Denys Turner (eds), *Silence and the Word: Negative Theology and Incarnation*. Cambridge: Cambridge University Press, 2002.

Dexter, Colin. *The Remorseful Day*. London: Macmillan, 1999.

Dexter, Colin. *Death is Now my Neighbour*. London: Macmillan, 1996.

Dillard, Annie. *Living by Fiction*. New York: Harper, 1982.

Dilley, Kimberly J. *Busybodies, Meddlers, and Snoops: The Female Hero in Contemporary Women's Mysteries*. Westport, Conn.: Greenwood Press, 1998.

Dubus, Andre. *Broken Vessels*. Boston: David R. Godine, 1991.

Bibliography

Eco, Umberto. *The Name of the Rose*. San Diego: Harcourt Brace, 1980 ('Postscript' in paperback edition, 1994).

Eliot, George. *Middlemarch*, ed. Rosemary Ashton. London: Penguin, 1994.

Ferreter, Luke. *Towards a Christian Literary Theory*. London: Palgrave, 2003.

Fiddes, Paul S. *Freedom and Limit: A Dialogue between Literature and Christian Doctrine*. Macon Ga.: Mercer University Press, 1999.

Freud, Sigmund. *The Interpretation of Dreams*, trans. James Strachey. New York: Avon, 1965.

Gardner, John. *On Moral Fiction*. New York: Basic Books, 1978.

Gidez, Richard B. *P. D. James*. Boston: Twayne, 1986.

Gladstone, William E. *The State in its Relations with the Church*. London: John Murray, 1838.

Gore, Charles (ed.). *Lux Mundi: A Series of Studies in the Religion of the Incarnation*. Cambridge: Cambridge University Press, 1889.

Grant, George. *Lament for a Nation: The Defeat of Canadian Nationalism*. Toronto: McClelland & Stewart, 1970 [1965].

Guardini, Romano. *The Spirit of the Liturgy*, trans. Ada Lane. New York: Benzinger, 1931.

Hadley, Mary. *British Women Mystery Writers: Authors of Detective Fiction with Female Sleuths*. Jefferson, NC: McFarland & Co., 2002.

Hansen, Ron. *A Stay against Confusion: Essays on Faith and Fiction*. New York: HarperCollins, 2001.

Harkness, Bruce. 'P. D. James', in *Art in Crime Writing: Essays in Detective Fiction*, ed. Bernard Benstock, 119–41. New York: St Martin's Press, 1983.

Hart, David Bentley. *The Beauty of the Infinite: The Aesthetics of Christian Truth*. Grand Rapids, Mich.: William B. Eerdmans, 2003.

Herbert, Rosemary. 'A mind to write', *Armchair Detective: A Quarterly Journal Devoted to the Appreciation of Mystery* 19/1 (1986): 340–8.

Herbert, Rosemary. *The Fatal Art of Entertainment: Interviews with Mystery Writers*. Toronto: Maxwell Macmillan Canada, 1994.

Horsley, Lee. *Twentieth-Century Crime Fiction*. Oxford: Oxford University Press, 2005.

Hubly, Erlene. 'The formula challenged: the novels of P. D. James', *Modern Fiction Studies* 29/3 (1983): 511–21.

Bibliography

Jackson, Christine A. *Myth and Ritual in Women's Detective Fiction.* Jefferson, NC: McFarland & Co., 2002.

James, P. D. *The Lighthouse.* London: Faber & Faber, 2005.

James, P. D. 'Manners and murder: women detective writers as social historians', presented at the Margaret Howard Memorial Lecture, 15 May 2003, St Cross Building, Oxford.

James, P. D. *The Murder Room.* London: Faber & Faber, 2003.

James, P. D. *Death in Holy Orders.* London: Faber & Faber, 2001.

James, P. D. 'Murder and mystery: medical science and the crime novel', *Transactions of the Medical Society of London* 115 (1998–9), delivered at Ordinary Meeting, Monday, 22 February 1999.

James, P. D. 'The craft of crime writing', The Borges Lectures. London: Anglo-Argentine Society, 1999.

James, P. D. *Time to Be in Earnest: A Fragment of Autobiography.* London: Faber & Faber, 1999.

James, P. D. *A Certain Justice.* London: Faber & Faber, 1997.

James, P. D. 'The girl who loved graveyards', in *London After Midnight*, ed. Peter Haining, 31–48. London: Little, Brown and Company, 1996.

James, P. D. 'On being the prodigal son', in *Our Childhood's Pattern: Memories of Growing up Christian*, ed. Monica Furlong. London: Mowbray, 1995.

James, P. D. 'Review of *The Reason Why: An Anthology of the Murderous Mind*, edited by Ruth Rendell', *Sunday Times Books* (8 October 1995): Section 7.

James, P. D. *Original Sin.* London: Faber & Faber, 1994.

James, P. D. 'Dorothy L. Sayers: her novels today', *Seven: An Anglo-American Literary Review* 10 (1993): 19–30.

James, P. D. *The Children of Men.* London: Faber & Faber, 1992.

James, P. D. 'A very commonplace murder', in *Great Law and Order Stories*, ed. John Mortimer, 352–69. London: Bellew, 1990.

James, P. D. 'A very desirable residence', in *English Country House Murders*, ed. Thomas Godfrey, 329–37. New York: Mysterious Press, 1989.

James, P. D. 'The art of the detective novel', *The New Welsh Review* 2/1 (1989): 4–9.

James, P. D. *Bad Language in Church.* London: Prayer Book Society, 1989.

James, P. D. *Devices and Desires.* London: Faber & Faber, 1989.

James, P. D. *A Taste for Death.* London: Faber & Faber, 1986 (1987).

James, P. D. 'Great-aunt Allie's flypapers', in *An International Treasury of*

Bibliography

Mystery and Suspense, ed. Marie R. Reno, 198–216. New York: Nelson Doubleday, 1983.

James, P. D. *The Skull Beneath the Skin*. London: Faber & Faber, 1982 (1983).

James, P. D. *Innocent Blood*. London: Faber & Faber, 1980.

James, P. D. *Crime Times Three: Three Complete Novels Featuring Adam Dalgliesh of Scotland Yard: Cover Her Face, A Mind to Murder, Shroud for a Nightingale*. New York: Charles Scribner's Sons, 1979.

James, P. D. *Murder in Triplicate*. New York: Charles Scribner's Sons, 1979.

James, P. D. *The Black Tower*. London: Sphere Books, 1977 (1975).

James, P. D. *Death of an Expert Witness*. London: Faber & Faber, 1977 (1978).

James, P. D. *Unsuitable Job for a Woman*. London: Faber & Faber, 1972 (1974).

James, P. D. *Shroud for a Nightingale*. London: Faber & Faber, 1971.

James, P. D. with T. A. Critchley, *The Maul and the Pear Tree: the Ratcliffe Highway Murders, 1811*. London: Constable, 1971.

James, P. D. *Unnatural Causes*. London: Faber & Faber, 1967 (pagination from Warner Books edition, New York, 1982).

James, P. D. *A Mind to Murder*. London: Faber & Faber, 1963.

James, P. D. *Cover Her Face*. London: Faber & Faber, 1962.

James, P. D. 'Foreword', in Ron Miller, *Mystery! A Celebration: Stalking Public Television's Greatest Sleuths*, x–xi. San Francisco: KQED Books, 1996.

Klein, Kathleen Gregory. 'Truth, authority, and detective fiction: the case of Agatha Christie's *The Body in the Library*', in *Analyzing the Different Voice: Feminist Psychological Theory and Literary Texts*, ed. Jerilyn Fisher and Ellen S. Silber, 103–16. Lanham, Md.: Rowman & Littlefield, 1998.

Klein, Kathleen Gregory. *The Woman Detective: Gender & Genre*. 2nd edn; Urbana: University of Illinois Press, 1995.

Knight, Stephen Thomas. *Crime Fiction, 1800–2000: Detection, Death, Diversity*. New York: Macmillan, 2004.

Kotker, Joan G. 'The re-imagining of Cordelia Gray', in *Women Times Three: Writers, Detectives, Readers*, ed. Kathleen Gregory Klein, 53–64. Bowling Green, Ohio: Bowling Green State University Popular Press, 1995.

Kotker, Joan G. 'P. D. James's Adam Dalgliesh series', in *In the Beginning: First Novels in Mystery Series*, ed. Mary Jean DeMarr, 139–53.

Bibliography

Bowling Green, Ohio: Bowling Green State University Popular Press, 1995.

Kresge-Cingal, Delphine. 'Intertextuality in the detective fiction of P. D. James: literary game or strategic choice?', *Clues: A Journal of Detection* 22/2 (2001): 141–52.

Leonard, John. 'Conservative fiction(s): P. D. James' *The Black Tower*', *Journal of Australasian Universities Language and Literature* 83 (1995): 31–41.

Majeske, Penelope K. 'P. D. James' dark interiors', *Clues: A Journal of Detection* 15/2 (Fall–Winter 1994): 119–32.

Malmgren, Carl Darryl. *Anatomy of Murder: Mystery, Detective, and Crime Fiction*. Bowling Green, Ohio: Bowling Green State University Popular Press, 2001.

Marks, Pamela. 'Mine eyes open: anti-romance in P. D. James's *Innocent Blood*', *Clues: A Journal of Detection* 21/1 (2000): 73–86.

McCrum, Robert. 'P. D. James talks about God, realism and Agatha Christie', *The Observer*, Sunday, 4 March 2001.

Milbank, John, Graham Ward, and Edith Wyschogrod. *Theological Perspectives on God and Beauty*. Harrisburg, Pa.: Trinity, 2003.

Mosebach, Antje. '"A smell of the place should almost rise from the pages". P. D. James and London – An Interview', *Anglistik und Englishunterricht* 54 (1994): 173–86.

Muers, Rachel. 'Silence and the patience of God', *Modern Theology* 17 (2001): 85–98.

Nelson, Eric. 'P. D. James and the dissociation of sensibility', in *British Women Writing Fiction*, ed. Abby H. P. Werlock, 56–69. Tuscaloosa: University of Alabama Press, 2000.

Newman, John Henry. *The Idea of a University*, edited with introduction and notes by I. T. Ker. Oxford: Oxford University Press, 1976.

Nixon, Nicola. 'Gray Areas: P. D. James's unsuiting of Cordelia', in *Feminism in Women's Detective Fiction*, ed. Glenwood Irons, 29–45. Toronto: University of Toronto Press, 1995.

O'Connor, Flannery. *Collected Works*, ed. Sally Fitzgerald. New York: Library of America, 1988.

O'Hear, Michael, and Richard Ramsey. 'The detective as teacher: didacticism in detective fiction', *Clues: A Journal of Detection* 21/2 (Fall–Winter 2000): 95–104.

Bibliography

Paul, Robert S. 'Theology and detective fiction', *Hartford Quarterly* 6 (Spring 1966): 21–9.

Paul, Robert D. 'Theology and detective fiction', *Student World* 55/2 (1962): 186–95.

Pears, Ian. *An Instance of the Fingerpost*. London: Jonathan Cape, 1997.

Pla, Sandra. 'P. D. James: a new queen of crime', *Caliban* 23 (1986): 73–86.

Plain, Gill. *Twentieth-Century Crime Fiction: Gender, Sexuality and the Body*. Chicago: Fitzroy Dearborn, 2001.

Porter, Dennis. 'Detection and ethics: the case of P. D. James', in *The Sleuth and the Scholar: Origins, Evolution, and Current Trends in Detective Fiction*, ed. Barbara A. Rader and Howard G. Zettler, 11–18. Contributions to the Study of Popular Culture, 19. New York: Greenwood Press, 1988.

Porter, Dennis. *The Pursuit of Crime: Art and Ideology in Detective Fiction*. New Haven: Yale University Press, 1981.

Pyrhönen, Heta. *Mayhem and Murder: Narrative and Moral Problems in the Detective Story*. Toronto: University of Toronto Press, 1999.

Richardson, Betty. '"Sweet Thames, run softly": P. D. James's *Waste Land* in *A Taste for Death*', *Clues: A Journal of Detection* 9/3 (1988): 105–18.

Reddy, Maureen T. *Sisters in Crime: Feminism and the Crime Novel*. New York: Continuum, 1988.

Rowland, Susan. 'The horror of modernity and the utopian sublime: Gothic villainy in P. D. James and Ruth Rendell', in *The Devil Himself: Villainy in Detective Fiction and Film*, ed. Stacy Gilles and Philippa Gates, 133–46. Westport, Conn.: Greenwood, 2002.

Rowland, Susan. *From Agatha Christie to Ruth Rendell: British Women Writers in Detective and Crime Fiction*. Basingstoke: Palgrave, 2001.

Salwak, Dale. 'An interview with P. D. James', *Clues: A Journal of Detection* 6/1 (1985): 31–50.

Sanchez-Arnosi, Milagros. 'El crimen o la fascinacion por el enigma', *Cuadernos Hispanoamericanos: Revista Mensual de Cultura Hispanica* 464 (1989): 125–8.

Scaggs, John. *Crime Fiction*. London: Routledge, 2005.

Sheed, Wilfrid. *The Good Word and Other Words*. Harmondsworth: Penguin, 1980.

Siebenheller, Norma. *P. D. James*. New York: Frederick Ungar, 1981.

Bibliography

Sizemore, Christine Wick. 'The city as mosaic: P. D. James', in her *A Female Vision of the City: London in the Novels of Five British Women*, 152–87. Knoxville: University of Tennessee Press, 1989.

Sophocles. *Oedipus the King*, trans. Francis Storr. Loeb Library Edition. Cambridge, Mass., and London: Harvard University Press and William Heinemann, 1912.

Smyer, Richard I. 'P. D. James: crime and the human condition', *Clues: A Journal of Detection* 3/1 (1982): 49–61.

Spencer, William David. 'Religious mysteries', in *Mystery and Suspense Writers: The Literature of Crime, Detection, and Espionage*, ed. Robin W. Winks and Maureen Corrigan, 2: 1161–81. New York: Charles Scribner's Sons, 1998.

Suerbaum, Ulrich. 'Neues vom Krimi? P. D. James und die Veredelung des Detektivromans', *Anglistik und Englischunterricht* 37 (1989): 7–31.

Taylor, Charles. *Sources of the Self*. Cambridge: Cambridge University Press, 1989.

Thiessen, Gesa E. (ed.). *Theological Aesthetics*. London: SCM Press, 2004.

von Balthasar, Hans Urs. *The Glory of the Lord*, vol. I: *A Theological Aesthetics*, trans. Erasmo Leiva-Merikakis. Edinburgh: T. & T. Clark, and San Francisco: Ignatius Press, 1982.

Ward, Patricia A. 'Moral ambiguities and the crime novels of P. D. James', *Christian Century* 101 (1984): 519–22.

Weil, Simone. 'Reflections on the right use of schools studies with a view to the love of God', in *Waiting on God*, trans. Emma Crawford. London: Routledge & Kegan Paul, 1951.

White, Terry. 'No gore, please – they're British', *New York Times*, 9 October 1988, Section 7: 1.

Whittingham, Charlotte. 'Christian ritual and creed in Åke Edwardson's *Gå ut min själ*', in *Crime Scenes: Detective Narratives in European Culture Since 1945*, ed. Anne Mullen and Emer O'Brien, 113–24. Amsterdam: Radopi, 2000.

Wimsatt, Jr, W. K., and Monroe C. Beardsley. *The Verbal Icon: Studies in the Meaning of Poetry*. Lexington: University of Kentucky Press, 1954.

Winks Robin W. (ed.). *Detective Fiction: A Collection of Critical Essays*. Woodstock, Vt.: Countryman Press, 1988.

Bibliography

Winks, Robin W. and Corrigan, Maureen. *Mystery and Suspense Writers: The Literature of Crime, Detection, and Espionage*, 2 vols. New York: Charles Scribner's Sons, 1998.

Wroe, Martin. 'The Baroness in the crime lab. Interview [with P. D. James]', *Books and Culture* (March/April 1998): 14–15.